THE ICONIC JERSEY

THE ICONIC JERSEY

BY ERIN R. CORRALES-DIAZ

WORCESTER ART MUSEUM

g

Worcester Art Museum, Worcester, Massachusetts,
in association with D Giles Limited

BASEBALL X FASHION

The Iconic Jersey: Baseball x Fashion is made possible through the generous support from the Fletcher Foundation. Additional support is provided by the Arthur M. and Martha R. Pappas Foundation, Bill and Joan Alfond Foundation, Lunder Foundation-Peter and Paula Lunder family, Murray Family Charitable Foundation, Larry and Stacey Lucchino, Cynthia L. Strauss and Harry A. Sherr, and an anonymous donor.

This exhibition is sponsored by Samuel Adams, Country Bank, Gilbane Building Company, and Gatorade. Media partner is The Boston Globe.

This catalogue accompanies the exhibition *The Iconic Jersey: Baseball x Fashion* on display at the Worcester Art Museum, June 12–September 12, 2021.

© 2021 Worcester Art Museum

First published in 2021 by GILES
An imprint of D Giles Limited
66 High Street
Lewes, BN7 1XG, UK
gilesltd.com

ISBN: 978-1-911282-88-4

The exhibition was curated by Erin R. Corrales-Diaz, PhD, Assistant Curator of American Art

For D Giles Limited:
Copyedited and proofread by Magda Nakassis
Designed by Alfonso Iacurci
Produced by GILES, an imprint of D Giles Limited
Printed and bound in Europe

All measurements are in centimeters and inches; height precedes width precedes depth.

Front cover: Detail of G Yamazawa wearing the Heart Mountain Jersey, 2017. Photograph by Jillian Clark (Fig. 57).

Back cover: Detail of Flodin & Thyberg, Worcester Grays Player, ca. 1887–90, albumen print mounted on cabinet card (Cat. 10).

Frontispiece: Detail of Walter Iooss Jr., *Tony Scott and Garry Templeton, Dodger Stadium, Los Angeles*, 1979, archival pigment print (Cat. 73).

Page 6: Detail of Tabitha Soren, *Lonnie Chisenhall, Cleveland Indians*, 2013, unique tintype (Cat. 56).

Page 11: Models wearing MIZIZI baseball jerseys (Fig. 58).

Page 187: Detail of Tabitha Soren, *Marco Scutaro, San Francisco Giants*, 2014, unique tintype (Cat. 55).

Library of Congress Control Number: 2021903040

CONTENTS

DIRECTORS' FOREWORD

As we write the introduction to this catalogue, the construction of a new baseball stadium, Polar Park, is in full swing in Worcester's Canal District, just a mile and a half from the Worcester Art Museum. Beginning with the 2021 season, the newly minted Worcester Red Sox, affectionately dubbed the "Woo Sox," will take to the plate for the first time on their home field in the heart of the city. The arrival of this Triple-A affiliate of the Boston Red Sox gives further momentum to our city's current renaissance, as new life comes to downtown Worcester through the development and expansion of office spaces, hotels, and restaurants. We at the Worcester Art Museum want to be in the front row for the opening celebrations, and what better way to welcome the team than through an exhibition that explores the connection between America's favorite pastime and art.

Worcester, Massachusetts was a baseball town long before our art museum opened its doors in 1898. Since the mid-nineteenth century, games were organized by a broad spectrum of youth, amateur, industrial, collegiate, and professional leagues. Worcester even boasted a Major League team—the Worcester Worcesters (National League), also known as the "Brown Stockings" or "Ruby Legs"—for two years in the 1880s. In subsequent decades, other leagues have brought our city the Worcester Busters (1906–17), Worcester Panthers (1923–25), Worcester Tornadoes (2005–12), and Worcester Bravehearts (2014 to present)—to name just the most prominent teams.

The residents of Worcester have demonstrated an abiding affection for baseball and the city has also been the site of major achievements and noteworthy firsts in the sport. On June 12, 1880, Lee Richmond of the Worcesters threw the first perfect game in Major League Baseball against the Cleveland Blues. For those of us less versed in baseball lingo, this means that no players from the opposing team made it on base—an incredibly difficult feat. This historic game was played on the Worcester Agricultural Fairgrounds, also known as the Driving Park, now the location of Becker College. That same summer, the Worcesters also became the first Major League team to secure a no-hitter at home. On April 14, 1939, Red Sox legend Ted Williams hit his first grand slam home run in Massachusetts—not in Boston, but rather on Fitton Field in Worcester, at an exhibition game against the College of the Holy Cross varsity team. And in 2002, Worcester's Jesse Burkett Little League made it to the Little League World Series championship. Although they lost to a team from Louisville, Kentucky, they made state baseball history with the best ranking in Massachusetts youth baseball to date.

It should also be mentioned that baseball is linked to the arts in Worcester's history. The oft-recited comic ballad "Casey at the Bat" (1888) was written by Worcester's own Ernest Thayer, a *Harvard Lampoon* alumnus. Thayer published this beloved poem while writing for the *San Francisco Examiner*. Ultimately, he returned to Worcester to run his family's mills. Where Thayer applied his literary skill to the subject of baseball, Dr. Erin R. Corrales-Diaz, Assistant Curator of American art at the Worcester Art Museum, has brought a curatorial lens to the sport by exploring the status of the baseball jersey in American culture. In doing so, Corrales-Diaz scored Worcester another baseball first: the first exhibition on the intersection of baseball and fashion in an art museum.

Through her fascinating investigation of the baseball jersey and its evolution, Corrales-Diaz has uncovered countless artists and artisans who have dedicated their aesthetic skills to baseball and shaped the look of the game over time: garment and graphic designers, seamstresses, tailors, and even at-home DIYers. Moreover, she has traced the transformation of the classic baseball jersey from uniform to streetwear to high fashion. In doing so, its deep cultural significance becomes manifest. More than just a means of representing one's home team pride, the jersey—as Corrales-Diaz deftly demonstrates—also offers a visual medium for broaching discourse on some of our nation's most difficult issues. In jerseys designed by G Yamazawa in collaboration with Runaway and by MIZIZI, we encounter designers that understand the symbolic weight of this cultural icon and use it to both assert connectedness as a team or a nation and at the same time cast a critical eye on how particular groups have been and continue to be excluded from this unity. Such work has particular resonance at this tumultuous moment in American history, as we, alongside many institutions, look for productive ways to engage in dialogue about racial inequality and address the inequities of structural racism.

The Iconic Jersey: Baseball x Fashion has proven the extraordinary capacity of a great project to build community. We have been heartened by the outpouring of support this exhibition has garnered from our steadfast patrons as well as new friends. We are grateful for the generous loans made by the National Baseball Hall of Fame and Museum and the Smithsonian Institution, which undergird the show. As this exhibition contains many materials that are not held in museums, some of

the items on view were located through word of mouth and via networks of individuals who find inspiration in this topic. Other items came to us out of the magnanimity of designers and fans. To all who played a part in assembling this magnificent array of jerseys and baseball ephemera, we thank you. Furthermore, we would like to thank the exhibition's underwriter, the Fletcher Foundation. Additional support is provided by the Arthur M. and Martha R. Pappas Foundation, Bill and Joan Alfond Foundation, Lunder Foundation-Peter and Paula Lunder family, Murray Family Charitable Foundation, Larry and Stacey Lucchino, Cynthia L. Strauss and Harry A. Sherr, and an anonymous donor. This exhibition is sponsored by Samuel Adams, Country Bank, Gilbane Building Company, and Gatorade. Media Partner is The Boston Globe.

As we await the first pitch at Polar Park, we look forward to celebrating a summer of baseball on the field and in the museum.

Matthias Waschek
Jean and Myles McDonough Director

Claire C. Whitner
Director of Curatorial Affairs and James A. Welu Curator of European Art

ACKNOWLEDGMENTS

On August 17, 2018, when it was announced that the Boston Red Sox's Triple-A affiliate would move from Pawtucket, Rhode Island, to Worcester, Massachusetts, I could not fathom my involvement in this outstanding community. I am grateful for the opportunity to bring baseball into the world of design and fashion, and with that thank members of the Red Sox Nation for their support: Sarah Coffin, Gordon Edes, Larry Lucchino, Steve Oliveira, Janet Marie Smith, and Dr. Charles Steinberg.

This project began as a small kernel of an idea that blossomed under the Worcester Art Museum's director and senior leadership team. I am grateful to Dr. Matthias Waschek and Dr. Claire C. Whitner for encouraging this project and seeing value in work outside of traditional fine art frameworks. Gareth Salway, Mark Spuria, and Marnie P. Weir helped oversee the logistics of the exhibition, budgeting, and programming. And Marillyn Earley is indefatigable, listening to my exhibition pitch time and time again.

Many of my outstanding colleagues at the Worcester Art Museum made important contributions to this project. Elizabeth Fox, curatorial assistant for American art, fact-checked essays and assisted in image requests. Alison Rosenberg oversaw a complex loan exhibition during a global pandemic; Sarah Gillis guided me through the wild world of image rights; and Steve Briggs photographed several of the loaned objects. Rita Albertson and Eliza Spaulding provided their conservation expertise. Aileen Novick and Elizabeth Buck devised excellent programming in education and experience. Alex Krasowski set up countless development meetings; and Karmen Bogdesic, Nancy Jeppson, Marleen Kilcoyne, and Christine Proffitt all worked hard to underwrite this ambitious project. Richard Albion, Julieane Frost, Sarah Leveille, and Kim Noonan helped to promote this project.

I am indebted to the tireless efforts of Donna Cohen, Lisa McDonough, Harry A. Sherr, and Mark Thomashow. They became my cheerleaders, eager to see this project succeed. Their countless e-mails, phone calls, and Zoom meetings made this project better than I could have ever imagined. I thank you.

Financial support for this project comes from the Fletcher Foundation. Additional support is provided by the Arthur M. and Martha R. Pappas Foundation, Bill and Joan Alfond Foundation, Lunder Foundation-Peter and Paula Lunder family, Murray Family Charitable Foundation, Larry and Stacey Lucchino, Cynthia L. Strauss and Harry A. Sherr, and an anonymous donor. This exhibition is sponsored by Samuel Adams, Country Bank, Gilbane Building Company, and Gatorade. Media partner is The Boston Globe.

I owe a world of gratitude to Todd Radom. He enthusiastically responded to an out-of-the-blue e-mail and became an integral part of this project. Through his support, I came to meet more folks "who get it" regarding uniform aesthetics. I have been overwhelmed with the response from this community and I would like to acknowledge their assistance: Craig Brown, Peter Capolino, Andy Hyman, Paul Lukas, John Thorn, and many others. Of course, no work on baseball jerseys would be complete without acknowledging the influential work of Marc Okkonen. My copy of his *Baseball Uniforms of the 20th Century* is now well-worn and filled with countless notes.

I am grateful to our lenders to this exhibition. The National Baseball Hall of Fame and Museum were early supporters of this project, eager to help with baseball fever in Worcester. During my research trip to the Hall of Fame, I thank Sue MacKay, director of collections, for allowing me to look at numerous jerseys, many of which have ended up in this exhibition. And to Cassidy Lent, who went above and beyond to make sure I had everything I needed while at the Giamatti Research Center. Later, when it came time to gather images for publication, I am indebted to John Horne, who effortlessly handled my requests, all while largely working remotely because of the pandemic. At the Smithsonian National Museum of American History, I thank the curators of the sports collection, Eric W. Jentsch and Jane Rogers, and project assistant Hanna BredenbeckCorp for assistance in research and loan requests.

Many thanks also go to our Salisbury Cultural District partners, the American Antiquarian Society (AAS) and the Worcester Historical Museum (WHM). At AAS particular thanks go to Lauren B. Hewes and Christine Graham. At WHM, William Wallace and his colleagues provided research assistance regarding Worcester's baseball history. Worcester has always been a baseball town and the future has never looked brighter.

To our dedicated exhibition design team at ikd, Tomomi Itakura and Yugon Kim, I thank you for your conversations, patience, and creativity.

I would also like to thank Dan Giles and the team at D Giles Limited of Harry Ault, Alfonso Iacurci, Allison McCormick, Magda Nakassis, and Louise Parfitt for encouraging and shaping this beautiful book. It is a delight for baseball and fashion fans alike.

As this book was written during the COVID-19 pandemic, many of my loan and image requests were complex, and I want to thank the folks who went above and beyond to help make this project a success: Amy Stephenson and Will Ballantyne-Reid at Ashish; Jamie Franklin and Callie Raspuzzi at Bennington Museum; Jodi Haller; James Cachey from the Hesburgh Libraries at the University of Notre Dame; Donna Russo and Lorna Condon at Historic New England; Jonathan Mannion Photography and Marjoriet Gueche; Bleue-Marine Massard from Louis Vuitton Malletier; Lynn Bloom and colleagues at Mitchell & Ness; Paakow Essandoh and MIZIZI; Wesley G. Balla and Douglas R. Copeley at the New Hampshire Historical Society; Jared Yazzie of OXDX; Randall Thropp and colleagues at Paramount Studios; Lynn Smith Dolby at the Penn Art Collection; Liz Daus and colleagues at R. J. Liebe Athletic Lettering Company; Darren Romanelli and Jason Kletzky; Gabe Eng-Goetz of Runaway and G Yamazawa; Guy Davis at Saint Vincent College; and Kevin Martinez and Ben VanHouten from the Seattle Mariners.

I am grateful to family and friends who were able to assist and support this project remotely. In particular, I'd like to thank my parents, Nancy Henkel, Kory Rogers, Hannah Weisman, and Amy Torbert.

And last but not least, I thank my pinch hitter Jeremy Henkel for all his help and his keen editorial eye.

Figs. 1–2. Anika Orrock, *It's Been A While* (*Part 1 & 2*), 2017, ink and digital.

ROOTING FOR LAUNDRY

There is something special about the baseball uniform, a mystique that is hard to pin down. Whether we are looking at someone in a uniform or we are trying it on ourselves, it is the feeling of the fabric, the design on the cap and jersey, the colors, cut, and history of the outfit that all lend meaning to our relationship with the game.

Tom Shieber, Senior Curator,
National Baseball Hall of Fame and Museum

In baseball, few things came before the uniform. Nine innings came later. The overhand delivery came later. The fielder's glove came later. The uniform is one of the oldest elements of the game.

Craig Brown, *Threads of Our Game*

The evolution of the baseball jersey is a graphic time line. From the materials to colors to style of letters, numbers, and logo, it tells the story of a team and its place in history.

Janet Marie Smith, Senior Vice President of
Planning and Development, Los Angeles Dodgers

The baseball jersey is an iconic garment and not only on the field of play. Worn by others to signify their allegiance to a club or a shared sense of purpose, the jersey began in that very way: as firemen's shirts, differentiated by hose or hook-and-ladder company. In the 1840s and 1850s, before baseballists thought to align themselves with their social clubs in this way, firemen wore shirts of red or white or blue, differentiated by the button-on bibs bearing the logos or initials or numerals of their fire company. The bib entered baseball in the 1850s and was gone by the 1880s, but the principal feature of the baseball jersey is unchanged: it shows that the wearer *belongs*.

John Thorn, Official Historian,
Major League Baseball

In my career as founder of Mitchell & Ness, I tried to represent the history of Major League Baseball through the evolution of the uniforms. The baggy wool flannels of 1876–1970 were emblematic of the utilitarian work ethic of American labor that built this country. The hip, new, tight-fitting double knits from 1970 to the present are fashion statements as well as colorful examples of our ever-changing tastes.

When the uniforms became a preferred outfit in the entertainment industry on MTV, VH1, and BET, people thought it was just a fashion statement of the time. It was not so much a fashion statement as a hearkening back to childhood memories. I know many of the artists were just kids at heart in love with baseball when maybe it was not cool, but they wore those colorful uniforms anyway.

Peter Capolino, Founder, Mitchell & Ness

Fig. 3. Anika Orrock, *Roberto Clemente*, 2018, ink and digital.

One of the first organized sports in America to equip players with uniforms, the baseball jersey often transcends sports, giving the player a sense of belonging, of community often leading to a greater sense of self.

Jane Rogers, Curator, Sports Collection, Smithsonian National Museum of American History

A baseball jersey shows a sense of belonging, you are part of a team. It feels like a sense of accomplishment and pride. It is also a part of history. Each jersey tells a story about a player, a team, a time in history.

Leslie A. Heaphy, Associate Professor of History, Kent State University, and Author of *The Negro Leagues, 1869–1960*

I still remember how getting my first Little League uniform made me feel so "official." Nearly half a century later, a baseball jersey still confers a special feeling of status upon anyone who wears it, from the biggest MLB star to the littlest T-ball player, and all the countless fans in between.

Paul Lukas, *Uni Watch*

Fig. 4. Anika Orrock, *Isabel "Lefty" Álvarez* from *The Incredible Women of the All-American Girls Professional Baseball League*, 2019, digital.

I put on my uniform and thought I died and went to heaven. Then, there was the music to my ears of the clickety-clack of my cleats. My dream came true.

Maybelle Blair, All-American Girls Professional Baseball League

It was 1970, I was a 13-year-old girl, and my coach handed me a purple box. Inside was my uniform; a white T-shirt with "The Pearls" in purple and a big number 8, purple stirrup socks, and purple shorts. I swear to God if I could be buried in that uniform I would.

Kat D. Williams, Professor of History, Marshall University, and Author of *Isabel "Lefty" Álvarez: The Improbable Life of a Cuban American Baseball Star*

The tunic dress uniform of the All-American Girls Professional Baseball League is one of the most visually iconic in baseball. It's immediately indicative of a time and place in American culture and society, but also uniquely representative of a significant chapter in the presence and journey of women in baseball. Over six hundred women who wore it utilized their professional baseball experience and salaries to blaze trails for generations of girls and women to follow. The incredible irony of this overtly feminine and completely impractical garment is that America's first (and so far, only) professional women's baseball league would not have been successful—and may not have existed—without it.

Anika Orrock, Illustrator and Author of
*The Incredible Women of the All-American Girls
Professional Baseball League*

Baseball is a sport that lends itself to introspection. The baseball jersey—officially elevated to art form here—has the power to span the ages and connect us to memories of so much—teams, players, ballparks, and the people we experienced those memories with.

Todd Radom, Graphic Designer and Author of
*Winning Ugly: A Visual History of the Most
Bizarre Baseball Uniforms Ever Worn*

Working in TV production, the shows used to give all sorts of swag to cast and crew. T-shirts, hoodies, and jackets were common premiums. A favorite was always the baseball jersey. There's something about a baseball jersey that connects that nostalgia to a sense of pride.

Lauren Meyers, Director,
The Other Boys of Summer

As baseball uniforms have moved from function to fashion, they have mirrored our changing tastes and trends. Most importantly, however, they represent a point of pride and unity for cities and towns, for Little Leaguers and Big Leaguers, who are proud to wear these garments of unity that proclaim our love for our team and our city. We will be thrilled if our jerseys become such a catalyst for Worcester.

Dr. Charles Steinberg,
President, Worcester Red Sox

Like baseball itself, American history is reflected in its baseball jerseys, from the flannels of the 1920s to the double knits of the 1970s to the cotton attire of the 2020s. Jerseys have an intrinsic excitement that can be seen at Fenway Park—and now Polar Park—on any given night. This celebration of the art of baseball jerseys is enlightening, enlivening, and inspiring.

Larry Lucchino, President and CEO Emeritus,
Boston Red Sox, and Chairman and
Principal Owner, Worcester Red Sox

The baseball jersey is like a fingerprint. It is indisputable evidence of who we are. That's as true for the players who wear them on the field as it is for the fan in the stands who roots for them. The players may fade with time but the uniform they wear never fades in our memories.

Dick Flavin, Poet Laureate of the Boston Red Sox

Fig. 5. Anika Orrock, *The Mudville Nine*, 2018, ink and gouache.

The outlook wasn't brilliant for the Mudville nine that day...

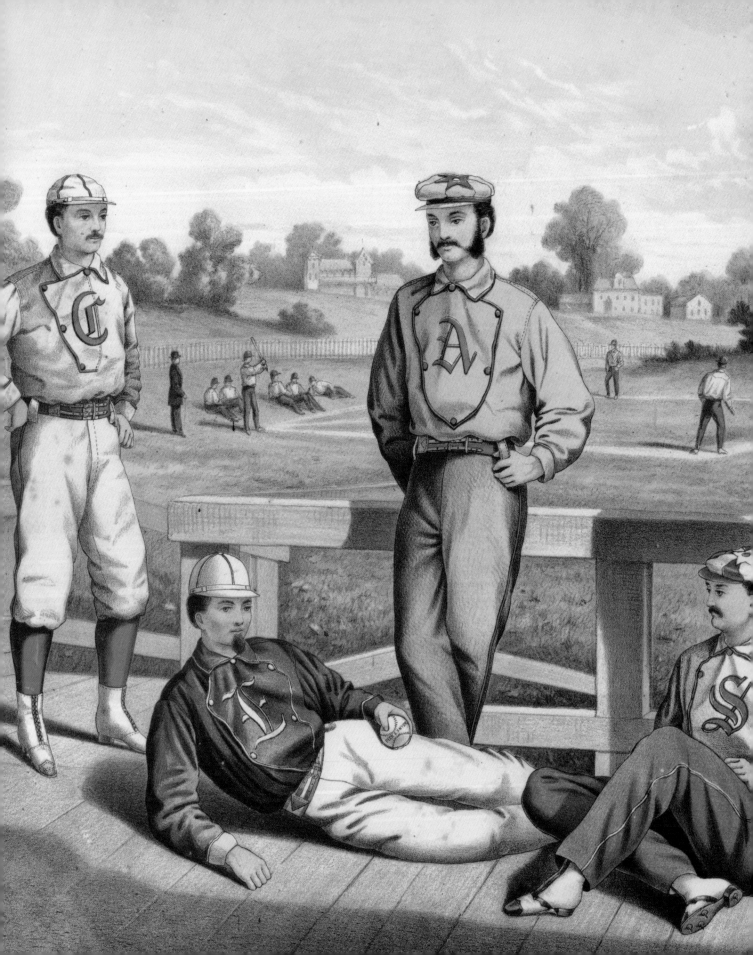

BEHIND THE SEAMS

Who are you wearing? This red-carpet question takes on a new meaning on the sports field for ballplayers and fans alike, especially when talking about team jerseys. Players may be traded or retire, teams relocate or change names, but for fans the uniform communicates their social identity, transcending the body of the individual athlete. As comedian and noted New York Mets fan Jerry Seinfeld famously joked about fans and their dedication to teams in spite of annual changes to their rosters: "We're screaming about laundry."[1] This is particularly apparent in cases when players upset fan expectations. The jersey becomes the medium for expressing outrage. When Milwaukee Brewer Ryan Braun admitted to using performance-enhancing substances, one fan notably altered her Braun jersey to read "Fraud."[2] And there have been several instances when fans modified or even burned a player's jersey.[3] It is a potent sociocultural emblem that rises above the significance of individual players or even the body. Notably, it is not the ubiquitous baseball cap that holds this kind of visceral and symbolic power. It's the jersey.

Since baseball's inception, uniforms—especially the shirt—have held significance by conveying a shared allegiance and sense of belonging. In 1869 Henry Chadwick, the "father of baseball," wrote in *Beadle's Dime Base-Ball Player*, "when a club is first organized, particular care should be taken to adopt a tasteful and appropriate uniform."[4] The uniform's shape and overall aesthetic connote unity, rivalry, and even excellence. Sporting goods manufacturer Draper and Maynard went so far as to proclaim that "a well-dressed team is a winning team."[5] Each baseball season, fans eagerly anticipate the unveiling of new uniforms, often presented through elaborate productions and runway shows with the players serving as models. This long-established tradition is evident in E. Butterick & Co.'s clothing advertisement from 1870 (Fig. 6). Aware of the scrutiny around uniforms, most teams hire design firms to develop a visual brand, one that will resonate with the community and prompt swift merchandise sales.[6] Critiques of each year's uniforms appear in editorials with discussions parsing the minutiae of stripes and logo placements. Of the uniform, the baseball jersey is the most visual and material representation of identity cultivation. As a result, jerseys are big business with licensed apparel sold to fans across the globe and teams wearing multiple uniforms over a season.

To don a baseball jersey is to engage in over 170 years of baseball fashion and design history. The origin of this significant garment begins with the

Fig. 6. (Detail) Engraved by John Schuller, published by E. Butterick & Company, *New York Fashions for March 1870*, 1870, chromolithograph, Library of Congress, Prints and Photographs Division.

New York Knickerbockers, primarily a social club for upper-middle-class New Yorkers that occasionally engaged in recreation (Fig. 7). On April 24, 1849, the Knickerbockers made baseball fashion history. At a meeting, they agreed to wear "blue woolen pantaloons, white flannel shirt, [and] chip (straw) hats" as a uniform.[7] By wearing uniform clothing, the Knickerbockers initiated fashion as a defining feature of the sport, one that fostered a sense of unity among the players and ease of viewing for the spectators. Over the decades, the evolution of the baseball uniform has revealed an increased focus on the shirt: ties have disappeared; sleeves have shortened; collars have reduced in size; and embellishments of logos and numbers have appeared. As the shirt adapted to new trends and demands, the nomenclature changed as well. In the nineteenth century, "jerseys" often referred to outerwear sweaters, but by the 1920s, the press and sporting goods manufacturers began to adopt "jersey" as the preferred term for the shirt.[8]

Today the jersey is not only found on the diamond or in the stands, but on the street and the runway. From the covers of music albums to the crowds at Fashion Week, the baseball jersey has come to stand for more than an affiliation with a team or an individual player, but reflects a larger commentary about culture, identity, and status. Moreover, it can also be a tool to recall forgotten narratives, promote social change, and subvert the status quo. The potency of the jersey's cultural significance has come to the fore in this country's struggle with racism, gender discrimination, and class inequality. Whether that be through the uniforms worn by the players in the segregated Negro Leagues of the twentieth century (Fig. 8), stereotypical images of Native Americans used as mascots, displays of hypermasculinity,

Fig. 7. Knickerbockers and Excelsiors Base Ball Clubs, 1859, National Baseball Hall of Fame and Museum, BL-73.37.

No known photograph exists of the New York Knickerbockers in their 1849 uniforms, but similar uniforms appear in this photograph from 1859 with the Brooklyn Excelsiors.

Fig. 8. Indianapolis Clowns Team, undated, National Baseball Hall of Fame and Museum, BL-6345-90.

The Indianapolis Clowns played in the segregated Negro Leagues.

Fig. 9. A fan wearing a homemade Boston Red Sox jersey at the World Series, October 12, 1967.

or profit-driven apparel, the baseball jersey is far from the neutral attire it was intended to be. The jersey unifies and divides, and at the same time has sparked a lasting stylistic shift in how and why Americans engage with sportswear in the everyday.

Clothing is a profoundly personal art form, accessible and intrinsic to our daily lives. Much like other forms of visual expression, fashion—whether it be a mass-produced athletic uniform or a bespoke designer dress—conveys a plethora of social significance as much as it displays creativity and craftsmanship. Fashion often exists in an uneasy relationship with the art museum, frequently placed on the defensive to claim its status as art or design.[9] Such debates certainly inform this work, but they are not the primary questions at the root of this exhibition and catalogue. Instead of asking whether the baseball jersey is fine art, we instead should be asking how design informs the baseball jersey's far-reaching influence in society. The complex visual nature of the baseball jersey calls for a reconsideration of the garment, one that moves beyond documenting uniform changes or revering the relics of noted ballplayers to a celebration of its artistic nature.

Much like any other form of fashion, the baseball jersey is performative, complete with its own rules and lexicon. Baseball players are subject to strict regulations over their uniforms as a means of presenting the team as a single unit and as a code of conduct.[10] In the stands, fans model their idols by wearing replica jerseys. Among the spectators at the stadium exists a spectrum of jersey-wearing fandom: Hall of Famers, current players, and even personalized shirts. As a statement piece, the baseball jersey communicates an ideal bodily self to others to garner respect and a sense of belonging (Fig. 9).

Fig. 10. Jeremy Scott's Spring/Summer 2013 ready-to-wear collection featured a blue snakeskin baseball jersey dress.

Fig. 11. Racks of replica jerseys at the St. Louis Cardinals' team store in Busch Stadium.

To a fan, wearing a baseball jersey transforms the observer into a participant in the game, even from the comfort of a living room or sports bar. And this transformation is also psychological, often providing a rush of adrenaline or the euphoria of camaraderie.[11]

While baseball fandom provides unspoken rules for wearing a jersey, streetwear and high-end fashion operate in alternative registers. Rebelling against the expected and the social norm, streetwear offers a space for self-expression, sampling and remixing garments from several styles to create a fresh, new look and meaning. By freeing the baseball jersey from its original intended use, streetwear is the ultimate bricoleur, offering a stylistic dissent.[12] Similarly, high-end designers subvert the baseball jersey's function into imaginative garments rendered in luxurious materials or embellished with sequins (Fig. 10). The instantly recognizable features of the baseball jersey make it appealing for designers—so much so that several brands, such as Supreme, A Bathing Ape (BAPE), and DKNY, have devised their own jerseys. By stripping out Major League Baseball (MLB) associations and conceiving new logos, patterns, and materials, designers forge their own identities while solidifying the iconic stature of the baseball jersey.

A replica jersey refers to any copy of a professional player's jersey. Authentic jerseys, on the other hand, are made to the official specifications of regulation sportswear and are often more highly prized for their careful construction and attention to detail (Fig. 11). Vintage replicas can either be "retro," referring to teams still in existence but not their current style, or "throwback," jersey styles for defunct teams or leagues. Among jersey connoisseurs, the throwback garners the most cachet: "the more obscure the style, the better."[13] Their rarity and the specialized knowledge implied by throwback jerseys makes them the most highly sought-after for collectors. An unexpected outcome of throwback popularity is newfound awareness of non-major leagues, such as the All-American Girls Professional Baseball League and the Negro Leagues.[14] Although commodified as prepackaged nostalgia, throwback jerseys offer the potential to foster dialogue about historically marginalized groups and their place in baseball history. Moreover, they have the potential to serve as agents for greater awareness and possibly even social change as calls to action against historical injustices.

If we reframe the sportswear baseball jersey in the context of fashion and design, we can engage in aesthetic inquiries about its shape and style, its evolution and stasis, and the cultural significance of baseball and baseball-inspired fashion in society. Accessible and recognizable, yet often overlooked for its familiarity, the baseball jersey captures the imagination—from Little Leaguers to couture designers. What makes some baseball jerseys more appealing or valuable than others? Why does bad design matter? Alternatively, who determines what is "bad" or "good" design? How did the baseball jersey, a garment designed as a sporting uniform, transform into a fashion statement and platform to express creativity and social commentary? *The Iconic Jersey* explores these questions by unraveling the historical threads of the baseball shirt and examining the interwoven aesthetic stories of technological innovation, societal change, and the lure of nostalgia.

AT THE LETTERS:
GRAPHIC UNIFORMITY

In baseball, a pitch across the plate that reaches the batter's chest is often referred to as "letter high" or "at the letters," terminology that puts fashion at the forefront of the sport. Baseball jersey trimmings—colors, patterns, letters, numbers, and logos—all provide a sense of unity, identification, and panache to the uniform and the game. These visual components resonate with fans and signal specific teams, eras, and players, prompting loyalty and an emotional connection—so much so that alterations to jersey graphics often lead to unrest in a fan base. When Nike, the MLB's current official uniform supplier, unveiled their 2020 jerseys with the iconic swoosh on the chest, the logo's prominent placement sparked outrage among fans. Some decried the swoosh as an encroachment of advertising on the jersey's pure form—a response indicative of the nostalgic power of tradition.[15] Yet the appearance of the Nike logo perhaps gestures toward a future conception of the jersey, one that features a new array of graphics to be designed and interpreted.

Baseball's first professional club, the Cincinnati Red Stockings, sported a uniform that became a sensation (Fig. 12). Their white, flannel, bib-front

Fig. 12. The manager of the Cincinnati Red Stockings, Harry Wright, designed his team's uniforms for distinctiveness and performance.

Fig. 13. Gucci's Autumn/Winter 2018 ready-to-wear collection included a collaboration with Major League Baseball.

shirts and red trimmings with an Old English initial for the team's name set the standard for nineteenth-century baseball uniforms. In baseball's early years, the logo was synonymous with a team's name or nickname, as with the Old English *D* that is still used by the Detroit Tigers. The iconic interlocking *NY* of the New York Yankees originated in 1877 when Tiffany & Co. designed the monogram for part of the New York City Police Department's medal of valor.[16] In 1909 the New York Highlanders (eventually the Yankees) wore jerseys with the overlapping letters—a choice reputedly inspired by co-owner and former police officer William Devery.[17] The simplicity of interlocking monograms has led to their longevity and to their status as classics among baseball logos. The cultural significance of the monogrammed baseball logo caught the attention of Alessandro Michele, creative director for Gucci. Known for its interlocking double G, the fashion house collaborated with MLB on their pre-Autumn 2018 runway show (Fig. 13). The New York Yankees', San Francisco Giants', and Los Angeles Dodgers' monogrammed logos appeared on bags, shoes, and elaborate garments, transporting the icons from uniform identification to status symbol.

Fig. 14. OXDX, Dream Team Jersey, 2017, fabric and screenprint.

By the mid-twentieth century, baseball logos took on heightened importance with the emergence of television and licensed merchandise. In 1966 the MLB formed MLB Properties, which approved licensees, provided trademark protection, and collected royalties from licensed products. Logos took on a new importance as baseball delved into commercial ventures. This also led teams to acquire several logos—primary, secondary, cap only, mascot, and so forth. The prevalence of logoed mascots—Mr. Red, Mr. Met, Brownie the Elf, the Beer Barrel Man—peaked during this period. Coinciding with the postwar television age and a push toward commercialization, franchises sought to instill team loyalty through recognizable and marketable character logos. Among these brightly colored, identifiable characters is Chief Wahoo, the racist logo mascot of the Cleveland Indians. In 1947 Indians owner Bill Veeck commissioned Walter Goldbach of a local ad agency to update the logo in the period's popular cartoon style.[18] The logo, depicting a caricatured Native American with an oversize nose and grotesque grin, remained a staple in the Indians' visual branding until 2018. OXDX, a Diné-owned fashion label, designed the Dream Team Jersey to call out Native American misrepresentation (Fig. 14). As part of the #dechief movement, the jersey featured a cutout silhouette of the Indians' mascot, a powerful removal of a long-standing offensive image. As a social activist statement, the jersey pushed against a complacent majority and helped fuel momentum to eradicate the logo.[19]

While logos, both mascots and letters, serve as visual shorthand for teams, the jersey features additional visual components such as player and team names, patches, and numbers. Baseball is a numbers game, full of statistics like batting averages and total home runs, but one number captures the imagination and passion of the sport—the jersey number. Players are immediately associated with their numbers—Derek Jeter #2, Babe Ruth #3, Hank Aaron #44 (Cat. 46). For many ballplayers today, the number on the backs of their jersey is more than a means of identification, but a part of the sport's history. A player's number reflects individual preferences and tradition. For instance, single digits are reserved for position players; pitchers don double digits; and anything above fifty is considered less desirable, often referred to as "spring training numbers."[20] Although most players do not get to select their numbers, their symbolism inevitably takes on an emotional value or even superstition, with some traded players going so far as to pay new teammates for "their" number.[21]

Jersey numbers in the Major Leagues first appeared on the sleeves of the Cleveland Indians in 1916. Conceived as a means to enhance the fan experience through easy identification, it also required the purchase of a scorecard to match the player with his number.[22] Despite aspirations that the innovation would spread to other cities, the Indians scrapped the idea amid complaints about the numbers looking unprofessional and the expense of extra fabric and stitching. Digits made a comeback in 1929 when the New York Yankees announced that players would wear numbers on their backs, following the trend in other professional sports.[23] The numbering assignment was not arbitrary, but reflected the lineup's batting order.[24] By 1937 all MLB teams wore numbers on the back of their jerseys. This would remain the standard until 1952, when the Brooklyn Dodgers made uniform design history by adding red numbers to the fronts of their jerseys.[25] This eye-catching change would lead to the first "TV numbers," jersey modifications for living room fans, especially with the advent of color television.[26] Often seen as a uniform classic, the Dodgers' red numbers served a practical purpose while fulfilling basic design principles such as balance and contrast in the overall color scheme.

In 1939 the Yankees continued their numerical trends by "retiring" the first number in Major League Baseball—#4, in honor of Lou Gehrig. A retired number signifies a high honor in the sport and renders that number unwearable by future players.[27] This solidifies the player's legacy and memory around a number, often becoming a shorthand for the player. When Jackie Robinson stepped out onto Ebbets Field to play for the Brooklyn Dodgers, he wore #42. Robinson's historic milestone and stellar career led to the only league-wide retired number. So iconic are these double digits that a 2013 feature film about Jackie Robinson was simply titled *42*. On April 15, 1997, Jackie Robinson Day, Seattle Mariner Ken Griffey Jr. wore the number in place of his own after receiving special permission. Soon thereafter, MLB decided that all players would be allowed to don #42 on April 15th in tribute to Robinson. 42's jersey also features in Spike Lee's 1989 film, *Do the Right Thing* (Fig. 15). Mookie, the film's protagonist played by Lee, wears a Jackie Robinson jersey to signify the character's complex position in an interracial 1980s Brooklyn neighborhood. But the jersey also held personal associations for the filmmaker, who, like Robinson, faced racism and dismantled the color barrier in his profession.[28]

The sartorial importance of numerical design on the jersey has not been lost on designers outside of sports clothing. The graphic nature and symbolism of the uniform number provides fashion designers a space to highlight their own numerical significance. For many designers, the double digits either represent the founding year of the fashion house or brand (Dolce & Gabbana and BAPE; Cat. 103) or the year of the collection (KTZ). For streetwear brands seeking to draw awareness to underrepresented histories, the uniform number acts as symbolic restitution and can redress distorted narratives. Streetwear company Runaway, based in Durham, North Carolina collaborated with rapper G Yamazawa to honor the Japanese American baseball players who continued to play ball while incarcerated during World War II (Cat. 105). One camp in Wyoming, the Heart Mountain Relocation

Fig. 15. © 1989 Universal.
Spike Lee in the film *Do the Right Thing*, 1989.

Center, had an active baseball team as it gave the prisoners with a diversion and solidified their American identity. Runaway x G Yamazawa's jersey uniform number reads "'42"—an abbreviation of the year the incarceration camp opened. The design of the baseball jersey and the utilization of player numbers provides a medium for messaging and self-expression within the realm of fashion.

MATERIAL MATTERS:
MAKERS AND MANUFACTURERS

Embedded within every stitch of a baseball jersey are the aesthetic stories of multiple hands and creators. From concept to execution and finally to the consumer, the baseball jersey of yesterday and today is not the result of a singular vision, but of many. From the large firms hired by franchises to devise an overall graphic identity to the sewers who construct the garments and add finishing touches, these are crucial moments of artistry and craftsmanship in the production of the jersey. Although baseball jerseys are largely mass-produced in factories, handmade elements persist. In this way, the baseball jersey shares a commonality with bespoke garments that further blurs the line between elite and popular fashion. The interest in these matters reflects the methodology of this exhibition and catalogue, one that is object-centered and based in the study of material culture.

Since the emergence of the modern sporting goods industry in the nineteenth century, manufacturers have negotiated the need to reach a wide distribution while still catering to the individual with "tailor-made" uniforms.[29] Draper and Maynard Sporting Goods Company, based in Plymouth, New Hampshire, started by making mitts for players and eventually expanded into uniforms. Salesmen would travel from town to town with material samples and catalogues, hawking their wares to local baseball teams. The in-person interaction and ability to feel the fabrics offered customers an assurance of quality and superior workmanship. A significant employer for the local New Hampshire population, Draper and Maynard hired men and women to sew, iron, and package the uniforms as part of a large chain of individuals from producer to customer (Fig. 16). Some uniform manufacturers outsourced the lettering and in 1923 the R. J. Liebe Athletic Lettering Company began in a Saint Louis basement with a pair of sewing machines (Cats. 32–42). The work caught the attention of Rawlings, who signed the family business to make the lettering for all of the major manufacturer's uniforms. Still in production today, the company is known for its elaborate, circular chain stitching on the St. Louis Cardinals' uniforms as well as several high-performance lettering adhesives and materials. Women, in particular, have a long history with the company, transferring the

Fig. 16. Men and women packing uniforms at the Draper and Maynard factory in Plymouth, New Hampshire.

patterns, inlaying the felt, and guiding the sewing machines.[30] Even major manufacturers, such as Majestic Athletic, which rely on computer-guided machines, engage workers in handwork techniques on the cutting-room floor and in constructing details like buttonholes and letter application. While tags or logos indicate only the manufacturer, there are many other unseen signatures of workers and designers who make baseball jerseys.

An appreciation of historical fabrics inspired the replica vintage jersey phenomenon. As most sporting goods manufacturers had shifted toward synthetics, flannels were no longer in demand. In 1978 Peter Capolino began repairing vintage game-worn jerseys and caps as part of his rebranded sporting goods company, Mitchell & Ness. While visiting a local manufacturer in 1985, Capolino stumbled upon a cache of discarded woolen flannels, which inspired him to begin making carefully researched and accurate throwback jerseys with the vintage material.[31] Three years later, Jerry Cohen discovered an abandoned pile of woolen baseball fabrics and founded Ebbets Field Flannels.[32] On opposite coasts, Capolino and Cohen independently had the same idea to establish businesses crafting authentic flannel baseball jerseys. Their stories are about the fabric and the obsessive quest for authenticity. Marketing to die-hard baseball fans interested in the meticulous accuracy of stitches, material, and graphics, the vintage replica jersey industry sells nostalgia and the celebration of age-old techniques in jersey construction. While Mitchell & Ness has expanded to include vintage jerseys made of synthetics, Ebbets Field Flannels remains firmly rooted in the woolen era of baseball (Cats. 94, 95, and 104). More than woven wool, vintage fabrics tell baseball's aesthetic history, one thread at a time.

Vintage baseball fabrics also inspired Los Angeles designer Darren Romanelli (DRx/Dr. Romanelli) to develop a distinctive style where he "performs surgery" on cast-off materials to suture together something new (Cats. 111–12).[33] A Frankenstein archivist of popular culture and fashion, Romanelli sifts through his collection of materials to transform what was old into unconventional, unique items. His deconstructed clothing, collectibles, and chairs indicate his deep interest in sustainability and passion for the natural wear and tear of older fabrics. Reflective of a larger movement in streetwear regarding the environmental impact of the fashion industry, Romanelli is revolutionizing ways to give life to discarded or overlooked materials. In the case of old jerseys, Romanelli is drawn to the iconography and the visual legacy of the team while he mixes and matches to reconstruct a garment imbued with history, creativity, and whimsy. Romanelli breaks the cyclic trend of modernity or tradition in baseball jerseys by envisioning sporting attire that exists both in the past and in the future.

The Iconic Jersey developed out of the move of the Boston Red Sox's Triple-A affiliate to Worcester and the city's construction of Polar Park Stadium. Eager to celebrate this monumental occasion for the city, the Worcester

Art Museum began to devise an exhibition by considering the most visual and symbolic aspect of baseball—the jersey. By using the jersey as a point of entry into aspects of society and culture, we can consider why we care passionately about sports attire and what such clothes mean to the world, without sacrificing aesthetic considerations. But what follows is not a comprehensive history of the baseball jersey, nor is it exhaustive in terms of its geographical scope (baseball has become an international phenomenon). Our approach was to highlight major moments in design over baseball's 170 years and include fashion representatives of the jersey's transformation into a social icon. The goal is to reconceive what we think of as worthy of art historical consideration and to emphasize the design and fashion of everyday objects all around us. In this project, high fashion resides beside sportswear, the mass-produced next to the bespoke, and the ephemera of manufacturer's catalogues and order sheets alongside the garments, emphasizing the interconnectivity between objects and design.

This catalogue is divided into three sections that allow for aesthetic rumination and intellectual curiosity. "The Modern Jersey" sets the stage for the aesthetic contextualization of the baseball jersey. In tracing the graphic time line of artistic choices in baseball uniforms, it is apparent that tradition and nostalgia still outweigh functionality. "Experimental Design" examines sartorial decisions that deviate from the traditional jersey shape. From practical modifications to the superfluous, these jersey alterations illustrate fashion trends and potential future evolutions. The final section, "Off the Field," looks at how the baseball jersey became the ultimate symbol of fandom and its emergence in luxury design and streetwear. Each of these themes explores the mediation of form and function and, in so doing, calls attention to sportswear and the power of its aesthetic appeal. In presenting an alternative reading of the baseball jersey, one that resonates in today's visual era, *The Iconic Jersey* reveals the long-standing collaborative intersection of baseball and fashion.

PLATES

Fig. 17. Detail of Majestic Athletic, Seattle
Mariners Inaugural "Turn Ahead the Clock"
Shirt, worn by Sam Mejias, July 18, 1998,
polyester (Cat. 76).

THE MODERN JERSEY

Whether someone is a die-hard Red Sox fan or has never seen a live game, most North Americans have encountered the distinct shape and style of today's baseball jersey: a short-sleeved, collarless, button-down shirt with the player's name and number on the back. Certain design components read more obviously as classic baseball aesthetic—think of the New York Yankees' pinstripes or the swooping typography of the Los Angeles Dodgers—but all Major League Baseball (MLB) jerseys use the same shirt template.[1] As standard and consistent as the shape and design of the baseball jersey appears now, this has not always been the case. Envision flannel wool, vibrant Technicolor, shield fronts, and even ties—all at one point or another found their way to the baseball jersey. Often perceived as timeless, the baseball jersey underwent several transformations before settling on the recognizable design we associate with the sport today. Far from static, baseball jerseys move through cycles of nostalgia and fashion-forward modernity. But even as the jersey evolves, it holds tight to certain customs of dress and design, instilling a belief in the traditional form of the American-style baseball jersey— though contemporary sportswear designers are looking for a change.

The first official baseball uniform had little in common with the modern jersey. Although baseball was played before the mid-nineteenth century, it was the New York Knickerbockers in 1849 who adopted a standard uniform. No image of the team in uniform is known to exist, but accounts described the attire as "blue woolen pantaloons, white flannel shirt, [and] chip (straw) hats."[2] In baseball's early days, a question of respectability arose due to the sport's cultural background among the urban working class. Eager to align ball clubs with other fraternal organizations, teams adopted uniform designs from volunteer fire and militia companies, including flannel fabrics and a bib-style front. The Knickerbockers' blue and white wool flannel was a conscious design decision to sway public opinion and to support the club's professionalism.

A former pitcher, Albert Goodwill Spalding entered into the business of baseball with his brother, founding A. G. Spalding & Bros. in 1876. Initially beginning with baseballs, Spalding soon expanded to other gear, published guides and instruction manuals, and in 1877 became the exclusive uniform supplier for the newly formed National League. His sporting goods catalogues continued to advertise the bib-front jersey until 1893, but he also promoted new uniform advancements with lace-front and button-up jerseys. By the early twentieth century, Spalding claimed that nearly 90 percent of all professional

Fig. 18. Nike 2020 MLB uniforms.

and college ballplayers wore his uniforms.[3] Throughout the first half of the twentieth century, most ball clubs wore Spalding uniforms, but local manufacturers—such as Rawlings, Draper and Maynard, and Stall & Dean—supplied gear to regional clubs, reducing the impact of Spalding's monopoly.

But it was the button-front jersey that would become the iconic style for most of the history of baseball (with a few dramatic exceptions). Mirroring general trends in sportswear and menswear, the baseball shirt became more simplified and casual, removing any unnecessary trimmings, including the collar. John McGraw, the manager of the New York Giants and a former ballplayer, disliked the jersey collars, claiming they were "useless." In 1906 his team made history not only for their status as "World's Champions," but for collarless shirts. Critics were dismayed at the innovation, referring to the jerseys as "pajamas."[4] While the New York Giants first introduced the collarless jersey in 1906, it took a few more decades for them to become standard. Baseball teams would fully adopt the full-length, button-down, collarless jersey by the 1920s and 1930s.

While the jersey's shape remained consistent in the mid-twentieth century, the trimmings underwent noticeable changes as teams began to solidify their identities through aesthetics. In 1930 the Detroit Tigers deviated from their traditional Old English initial for uniforms with a slanted script. Most teams adopted the slanted letters, even adding a flourish underneath, rendering this lettering style inseparable from baseball. Consistent with consumerism and marketing trends of the mid- to late twentieth century, baseball teams embraced nicknames and formulated symbolic logos for their brand identities. Patches, logos, players' names, and numbers all appeared on the jersey during this time, rendering the garment a visual feast of iconography.

In 1970 the Pittsburgh Pirates changed their uniforms mid-season and ushered in a new era of the baseball jersey: the double knit pullover. Made of lightweight nylon- or polyester-blend material, the pullover offered players a respite from heavier fabrics and a more streamlined design. Those synthetic fabrics allowed for bolder, nontraditional colors and graphics than previous generations of ballplayers and fans had witnessed—perfect for color television. Fitting with the decade's significant social and technological changes, the vibrant double knit pullover represented the modern era, a garment far removed from the traditional button-down jersey. By 1972 most teams had adopted the double knit pullover, which became a staple in Major League Baseball for the next two decades.

When Rawlings became MLB's first official uniform supplier in 1987, they looked to the past for inspiration. Responding to Ronald Reagan–era conservatism, Rawlings issued new uniforms that abandoned the functional pullover for the traditional button-down jersey, which read as "baseball-ish."[5] Baseball jersey design of the late 1980s and early 1990s merged traditional shapes with modern fabrics and the occasional bold palette. *Sports Illustrated* noted the nod to tradition, writing: "At present, baseball is caught up in a wave of nostalgic fervor, a postmodernist period, designers might say. Teams are reaching into their pasts for a button here, a belt there, adding pinstripes, abandoning color, rehabilitating long-neglected symbols."[6] Awash with nostalgia, contemporary baseball jerseys speak more to a romanticization of the sport, an idea that what was will propel the sport and its fans into the future.

Yet sportswear designers claim that baseball's uniform is long overdue for a design overhaul.[7] One could argue that today's jersey is largely obsolete as most players wear a tight-fitting activewear layer underneath the oversize button-down. Such fashion choices can actually hinder players' performances, as the extra layers add weight during hot summer months and the oversize jersey provides drag resistance during dramatic slides. Even with Nike now leading the charge for uniform design in the Major Leagues, it looks likes convention prevails over innovation. The modern baseball jersey is here to stay—at least for now.

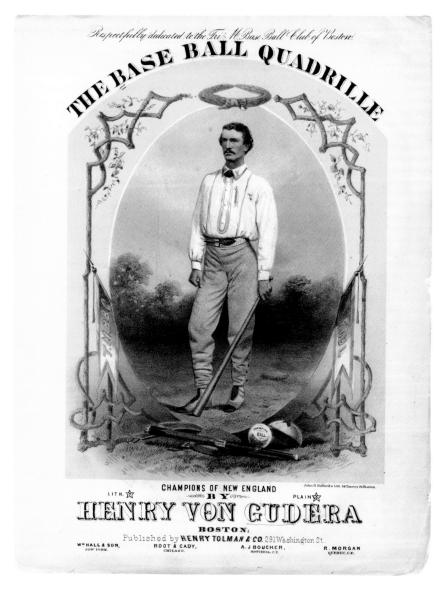

Cat. 1

Composed by Henry von Gudera
Lithography by John H. Bufford
(American, 1810–1870)
The Base Ball Quadrille, 1867
Colored lithograph
35 × 27 cm (13.78 × 10.63 in.)
American Antiquarian Society

Composer Henry von Gudera dedicated his 1867 song "The Base Ball Quadrille" to the Tri-Mountain Club of Boston after they won the top prize in the New England Association.[1] The Tri-Mountains wore an early uniform consisting of a white half-placket, or button-down, shirt with a decorative trim, a commemorative red ribbon over the left chest, and crossed bats sewn onto the collar points. Printed by the lithography firm of John H. Bufford and published by Henry Tolman & Co., this sheet music presents a rare example of a nineteenth-century jersey in color.

Cat. 2

Peck & Snyder
(American, founded 1866)
Advertising Broadside, ca. 1870s
Hand-colored wood engraving
36 × 56 cm (14³⁄₁₆ × 22 in.)
Reproduced from the original
held by the Department of Special
Collections of the Hesburgh
Libraries of Notre Dame
Catalogue only

In 1866 Andrew Peck and Ward B. Snyder joined forces to create the indomitable New York firm of Peck & Snyder, a prominent mid-nineteenth-century manufacturer of baseball supplies. This large printed advertisement, known as a broadside, depicts in bold color the uniforms and accessories available for purchase. Notable is the inclusion of a fireman's uniform (no. 34), as Peck & Snyder manufactured both fire company and baseball apparel. Despite the visual impact of the colored engraving, sometimes text and image did not match up correctly—the Boston player in the lower right is actually wearing a Cincinnati Red Stockings uniform.

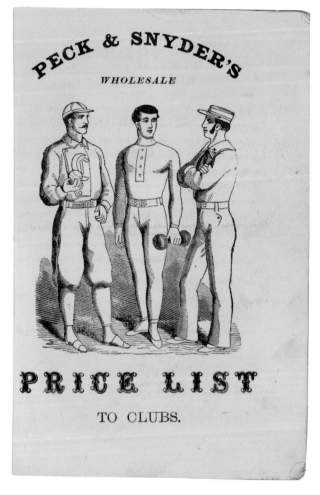

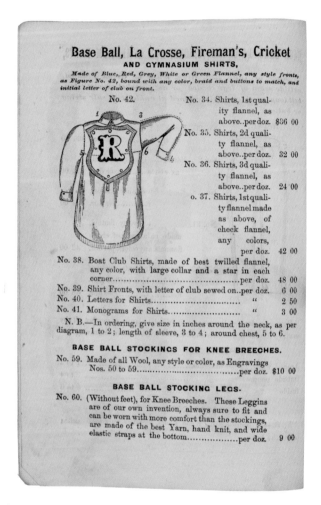

Cat. 3

Peck & Snyder
(American, founded 1866)
Peck & Snyder's Encyclopedia and Illustrated and Descriptive Price List of All Out- and Indoor Games; Also, Sporting Goods of Every Description, for the Use of All Whom It May Concern, ca. 1875
Reproduced from the original held by the Department of Special Collections of the Hesburgh Libraries of Notre Dame
Catalogue only

In addition to broadsides, Peck & Snyder issued annual encyclopedic catalogues of their wares with colored plates. Much like retailers today, manufacturers presented a range of offerings at different price points depending upon the level of customization and fabric quality. Although the shape of the shield varied from rectangular to fancy, Peck & Snyder primarily offered bib-front baseball shirts, a commercial strategy as the company also used the same patterns for firemen's uniforms. To demonstrate their ability and the quality of their uniforms, Peck & Snyder included colored plates of prominent baseball teams, such as the New York Mutuals.

No. 34. Firemen, (Dress Uniform.)

No. 31. Pastor (Tony Pastor,) B. B. Club.

Cat. 3b

A fireman's uniform features a bib-front devised for protection against debris or burning embers. Such a design was an inspirational source for early baseball jerseys.

Cat. 3c

The colorful uniform of Tony Pastor, a vaudeville star, who presented his skit, "Base Ball, or the Champion Nine," at his New York opera house in 1868.

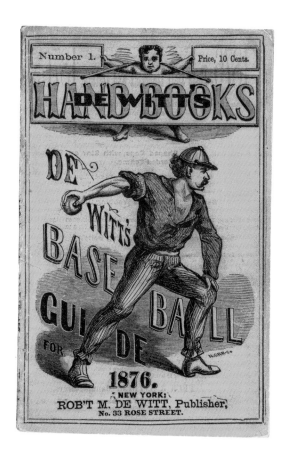

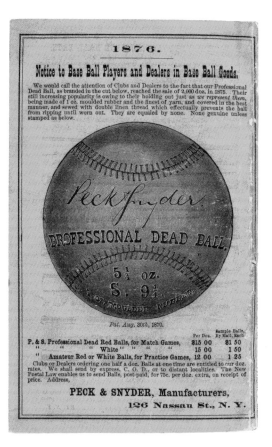

Cat. 4

Published by Robert M. De Witt
(American, 1827–1877)
De Witt's Baseball Guide, 1876
Woodcut on cover
16.5 × 10.5 cm (6½ × 4.2 in.)
American Antiquarian Society

Annual baseball guides offered sports
enthusiasts a statistical recollection
of the previous season and updated
rosters for the current year. New York
publisher Robert M. De Witt founded
De Witt's Baseball Guide in 1868
and hired Henry Chadwick, an early
authority on the sport, as its editor.
Given the popularity of these guides,
sporting goods manufacturers often
advertised their wares in the endpapers.
The firm of Nathaniel Orr engraved the
cover illustration of a pitcher with his
bib-front shirt partially unbuttoned.
The bib-style shirt offered players
flexibility for shifts in temperature:
an extra layer in the cold and removal
during warm weather.

Cat. 5

Harvard College Baseball Team, 1877
Albumen print on card mount
23.7 × 19.1 cm (9 5⁄16 × 7 ½ in.)
Historic New England

Variations of Harvard's first baseball club uniform—a button-up, bib-front shirt with an Old English *H*—were worn by players until 1882. Yet since 1876, that uniform was largely a nod to tradition with players donning tight-fitted, short-sleeved, worsted pullovers with a block *H* for actual games.[2] This photograph of the 1877 nine contrasts the ornate early uniforms with the simplicity of performance wear, illustrating the perpetual tension between tradition and innovation in baseball uniforms. In the center of the photograph is a metal catcher's mask, invented by the team's captain Frank Thayer (center left) and first worn by Jim Tyng (center right).

Fig. 19. Team portraits varsity baseball, 1876, Harvard University, Harvard University Archives, hua25013c00011.

An 1876 photograph of the Harvard club shows the players in a sleeveless version of the pullover.

43

Cat. 6

George H. Emery
(American, 1855–1930)
Burr and Burton Academy Baseball
Team, 1880s–1900
Photographic print on card mount
24.1 × 17.8 cm (9½ × 7 in.)
Bennington Museum, Estate of Roy
Estabrook, 1990.139.9

Burr and Burton Academy, a boarding
school and seminary located in
Manchester, Vermont, sported a
pullover-style shirt that could be used
for various athletics, including baseball.[3]
The short-sleeved, tight-fitting shirt
with the team's initials in block letters
offered players full range of movement
and flexibility necessary for a wide
range of sports. The pullover style
was sporadically adopted by ball clubs
throughout the nineteenth century, but
was often popular among the junior,
collegiate, and amateur leagues for its
affordability and versatility.

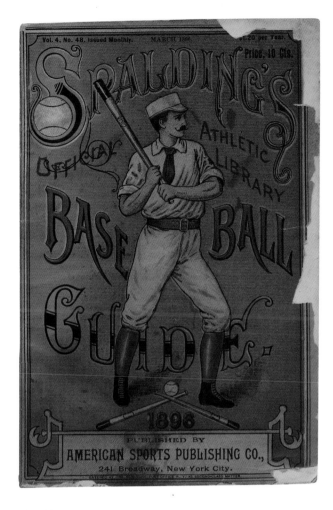

Cat. 7

American Sports Publishing Company
(American, 1894–1939)
Spalding's Official Base Ball Guide, 1896
Bennington Museum, Gift of Mrs.
Margery Ludlow, 1961.11

From 1877 to 1939, the American
Sports Publishing Company issued the
annual *Spalding's Official Base Ball
Guide*, serving as a compendium of
statistics, team rosters, and rules to
advance the playing and instruction
of baseball. The annual publication
also advertised Spalding baseball
equipment and uniforms in the back
matter. The 1896 edition included
a full page on Spalding baseball
uniforms, offering four different fabric
grades with shirts in both lace-front
and button-down styles. The cover
illustration depicts A. G. Spalding as
a player in 1876 wearing his Chicago
White Stockings uniform, complete with
a full-collar, half-placket button-down
and tucked-in tie.

Spalding's Base Ball Uniforms.

COMPLETE.

Including Shirt, Padded Pants, Cap, Belt and Stockings.

No. 0. *Spalding* Uniform $14.75
No. 1. "University" Uniform.......... 11.25
No. 2. "Interscholastic" Uniform...... 9.00
No. 3. "Club Special" Uniform....... 6.25
No. 4. "Amateur Special" Uniform.... 4.50

Our line of flannels for Base Ball Uniforms consists of the best qualities in their respective grades and the most desirable colors for Base Ball Uniforms. Each grade is kept up to the highest point of excellence and quality improved wherever possible every season. Owing to the heavy weight flannels used in our Nos. 0 and 1 Uniforms, we have found it desirable, after many years of experience, to use a little lighter weight material for the shirts; this makes them more comfortable, much cooler, and wear just as well as the heavier weight. If, however, you prefer the heavier goods for the shirts, they will be supplied at same price, but only when *specially ordered*.

Spalding's Base Ball Shirts.

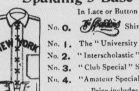

In Lace or Button Front.   EACH.

No. 0. *Spalding* Shirt, any style. $5.50
No. 1. The "University" Shirt, any style....... 4.50
No. 2. "Interscholastic" Shirt, any style 3.75
No. 3. "Club Special" Shirt, any style 2.50
No. 4. "Amateur Special" Shirt, any style....... 1.85
Price includes Lettering on Shirts.

Spalding's Base Ball Pants.

In Tape or Elastic Bottom. All Padded.   PAIR.

No. 0. *Spalding* Pants......................$6.00
No. 1. "University" Pants 4.50
No. 2. "Interscholastic" Pants..... .... 3.50
No. 3. "Club Special" Pants.... .... 2.50
No. 4. "Amateur Special" Pants............................... 1.75

COMPLETE CATALOGUE FREE.

Cat. 7b

An interior advertisement for Spalding's
baseball uniforms.

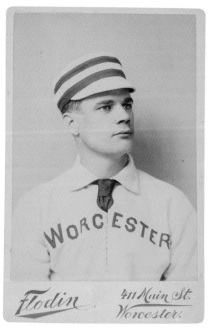

Cat. 8

Flodin & Thyberg (active
Worcester, 1887–95)
Worcester Grays Player, ca. 1887–90
Albumen print mounted on cabinet card
16.5 × 10.2 cm (6½ × 4 in.)
Courtesy of Central Mass Auctions, Inc.

Cat. 9

Flodin & Thyberg (active
Worcester, 1887–95)
Worcester Grays Player, ca. 1887–90
Albumen print mounted on cabinet card
16.5 × 10.2 cm (6½ × 4 in.)
Courtesy of Central Mass Auctions, Inc.

Cat. 10

Flodin & Thyberg (active
Worcester, 1887–95)
Worcester Grays Player, ca. 1887–90
Albumen print mounted on cabinet card
16.5 × 10.2 cm (6½ × 4 in.)
Courtesy of Central Mass Auctions, Inc.

Cat. 11

Flodin & Thyberg (active
Worcester, 1887–95)
Worcester Grays
Player, ca. 1887–90
Albumen print mounted
on cabinet card
16.5 × 10.2 cm (6½ × 4 in.)
Courtesy of Central Mass
Auctions, Inc.

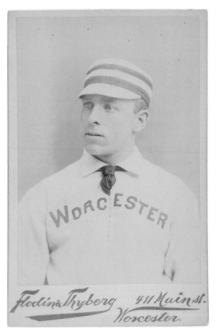

Cat. 12

Flodin & Thyberg (active
Worcester, 1887–95)
Worcester Grays Player, ca. 1887–90
Albumen print mounted on cabinet card
16.5 × 10.2 cm (6½ × 4 in.)
Courtesy of Central Mass Auctions, Inc.

Cat. 13

Flodin & Thyberg (active
Worcester, 1887–95)
Worcester Grays Player, ca. 1887–90
Albumen print mounted on cabinet card
16.5 × 10.2 cm (6½ × 4 in.)
Courtesy of Central Mass Auctions, Inc.

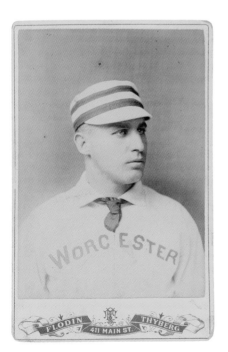

Cat. 14

Flodin & Thyberg (active
Worcester, 1887–95)
Worcester Grays Player, ca. 1887–90
Albumen print mounted on cabinet card
16.5 × 10.2 cm (6½ × 4 in.)
Courtesy of Central Mass Auctions, Inc.

A minor league team, the Worcester
Grays existed from 1879 to 1890. Likely
named for the color of their flannels,
the Grays wore collared, lace-front
shirts in flannel with a tie tucked into
the placket. A popular accessory in the
mid-nineteenth century, ties reflected
a standard of formal dress during the
period and strengthened the sport's
association with elite respectability.
Indicative of the late nineteenth-century
shift toward displaying the team's city
on the shirt, the Grays' jerseys have
block, felt letters of "Worcester" arched
across the chest. In a convergence
of sports and the arts, Worcester
photographers Ferdinand Flodin and
August Thyberg took portraits of the
players in their downtown studio. A
predecessor of today's baseball cards,
cabinet cards were primarily taken for
family and friends rather than for the
public or for promotional purposes.

Cat. 15

Wright & Ditson
(American, founded 1871)
Boston Red Sox Uniform Shirt, worn by
Jesse Tannehill, 1908
Wool flannel
86.4 × 63.5 cm (34 × 25 in.)
National Baseball Hall of Fame and
Museum, B-176-61

On opening day in 1908, the newly
christened Boston Red Sox (previously
the Americans) adopted red trimmings
with a distinctive and thoroughly
modern logo: a red sock with "Boston"
written in gray flannel. The red sock
connotes the team's nickname without
the need for text. Yet this semiotic
branding was ahead of its time. By
December of that year, the logo was
discarded: "The flaring bit of red flannel
in the form of sock that decorated the
shirt fronts of the players on the Boston
American baseball team is doomed.
All that will be left next season is the
memory of that flagrant object."[4]

Fig. 20. Cy Young of the Boston Red
Sox on Cy Young Day, 1908, Boston
Public Library, Michael T. "Nuf Ced"
McGreevy Collection.

On August 13, 1908, Cy Young wore his
jersey to a celebration in his honor.

Fig. 21. Michael T. McGreevy presents
diamond ring to Amby McConnell, Boston
Red Sox Spring Training, 1909, glass
negative, Boston Public Library, Michael
T. "Nuf Ced" McGreevy Collection.

During the Red Sox's spring training for
the 1909 season, players wore a variety of
old uniforms, including the previous year's
logoed jersey.

Cat. 16

Sherborn Athletic Association Baseball
Team, ca. 1900s
Photographic print on card mount
20.5 × 15.6 cm (8 ¹⁄₁₆ × 6 ⅛ in.)
Historic New England

As baseball clubs formed in towns
throughout twentieth-century America,
amateur teams donned their uniforms
with pride. Many sporting goods
manufacturers such as A. G. Spalding
offered various fabric grades and
pricing tiers that enabled teams from all
leagues to purchase complete uniforms.
The Sherborn Athletic Association
players wore button-front jerseys
with fold-down collars and the team's
initials in block letters, typical of the
movement toward simplicity in early
twentieth-century uniform design.

WADDELL. ST. LOUIS AMER.

DONOHUE. CHICAGO AMER.

HERZOG, N. Y. NAT'L

Cat. 17

American Tobacco Company
(American, 1890–94)
Rube Waddell Tobacco Card, 1909–11
Halftone and chromolithograph
6.4 × 3.8 cm (2½ × 1½ in.)
Bennington Museum, Gift of
Mrs. Ludlow, 1956.404.4

Early baseball cards were
advertisements for tobacco companies
designed to entice consumers to
collect entire sets, thus ensuring
brand loyalty. Printed by the American
Tobacco Company and distributed
among sixteen cigarette brands, the
"white border" series (T206) were
the most colorful baseball cards to
date, incorporating both halftone and
chromolithographic printing processes.[5]

Cat. 18

American Tobacco Company
(American, 1890–94)
Jiggs Donohue Tobacco Card, 1909–11
Halftone and chromolithograph
6.4 × 3.8 cm (2½ × 1½ in.)
Bennington Museum, Gift of
Mrs. Ludlow, 1956.404.9

Unlike earlier baseball cards, this
series offered depictions of players in
action, which revealed how the jersey
fit and moved on the body. Indicative
of the early twentieth century, these
cards exhibit the preferred design of
the era: a half-placket button-down.
The cards served as an important
means of visually distributing uniform
designs to fans, many of whom had only
experienced them through black-and-
white photography.

Cat. 19

American Tobacco Company
(American, 1890–94)
Buck Herzog Tobacco Card, 1909–11
Halftone and chromolithograph
6.4 × 3.8 cm (2½ × 1½ in.)
Bennington Museum, Gift of
Mrs. Ludlow, 1956.404.8

Buck Herzog's New York Giants
jersey illustrates the sun collar, or
a "collarless" V-neck with a small
extension of fabric intended to shield
players from the sun.

Cat. 20

Spalding (American, founded 1876)
Chicago Cubs Uniform Shirt, worn by
Johnny Kling, 1909
Wool flannel
78.7 × 58.4 cm (31 × 23 in.)
National Baseball Hall of Fame and
Museum, B-175-59

In 1909 the Chicago Cubs debuted their
new road uniforms designed by A. G.
Spalding & Bros., sparking a short-lived
trend. Instead of a fold-over collar, the
Cubs sported a military-inspired cadet
or "standing" collar that fastens at the
throat. This jersey marks the first time
a full team name (city and nickname)
appeared on a Major League baseball
uniform. Chicago reads vertically down
the front placket and an insignia with
an oversize C encircles the rest of the
team's name. This early design is the
origin of the Cubs logo today.

Fig. 22. Chicago Daily News, Inc., Chicago
Cubs Player Mordecai Brown, 1909, glass
negative, Chicago History Museum, Chicago
Daily News Collection, 1960.784.

Pitcher Mordecai Brown wearing the
Chicago Cubs road uniform in 1909.

3088-6

KEIO UNIVERSITY BALL TEAM

Fig. 23. Keio University Ball Team, April 22, 1914, glass negative, Library of Congress Prints and Photographs Division, George Grantham Bain Collection, LC-B2-3088-6.

Members of the White Sox, Giants, and Japan's Keio University baseball teams during a world tour on April 22, 1914.

Cat. 21

Spalding (American, founded 1876)
Chicago White Sox Uniform Shirt, worn by Urban "Red" Faber, 1914
Wool flannel
120 × 92.1 cm (47¼ × 36¼ in.)
National Baseball Hall of Fame and Museum, B-613-64

The Chicago White Sox and the New York Giants embarked on a yearlong world tour following the 1913 World Series. This A. G. Spalding jersey was likely one of several nationally inspired uniforms worn by players as they traversed the globe. Drawing inspiration from military uniforms, the jersey features a cadet collar with red and blue trimmings and unfurling American flags gracing the sleeves. Such bold color contrasts and patriotic insignia on the button-front jersey conveyed America's strength and power on the field and around the globe. The jersey also features underarm ventilation gussets in the sleeves, an invention designed for comfort and increased movement that Spalding introduced in 1911.[6]

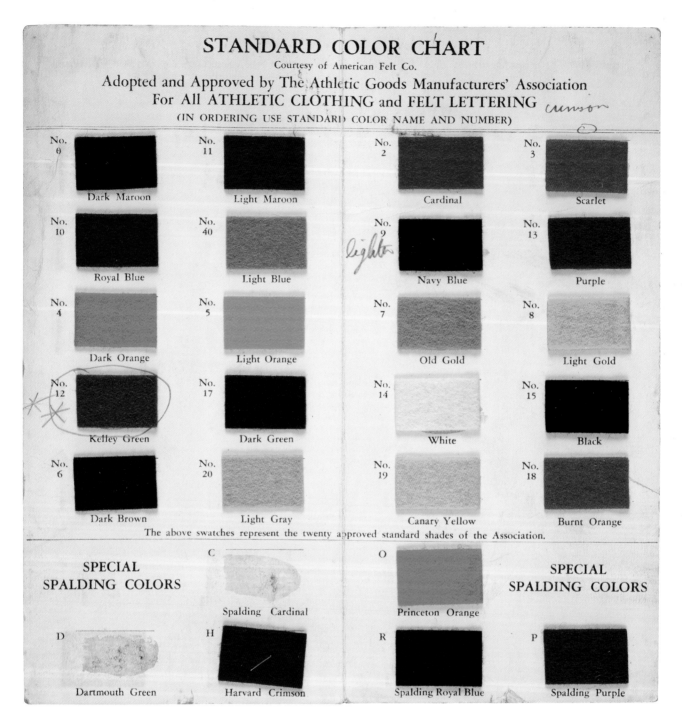

STANDARD COLOR CHART

Courtesy of American Felt Co.

Adopted and Approved by The Athletic Goods Manufacturers' Association
For All ATHLETIC CLOTHING and FELT LETTERING *crimson*

(IN ORDERING USE STANDARD COLOR NAME AND NUMBER)

No. θ Dark Maroon	No. 11 Light Maroon	No. 2 Cardinal	No. 3 Scarlet
No. 10 Royal Blue	No. 40 Light Blue	No. 9 Navy Blue	No. 13 Purple
No. 4 Dark Orange	No. 5 Light Orange	No. 7 Old Gold	No. 8 Light Gold
No. 12 Kelley Green	No. 17 Dark Green	No. 14 White	No. 15 Black
No. 6 Dark Brown	No. 20 Light Gray	No. 19 Canary Yellow	No. 18 Burnt Orange

The above swatches represent the twenty approved standard shades of the Association.

SPECIAL SPALDING COLORS

C Spalding Cardinal

O Princeton Orange

SPECIAL SPALDING COLORS

D Dartmouth Green

H Harvard Crimson

R Spalding Royal Blue

P Spalding Purple

Cat. 22

Spalding (American, founded 1876)
Athletic Goods Manufacturers'
Association Standard Color Chart, 1920
Paper and felt
Closed: 19.1 × 8.3 cm (7½ × 3¼ in.)

In 1906 six sporting goods manufacturers met in New York City to form the Athletic Goods Manufacturers' Association to "create better feelings and good fellowship among the manufacturers."[7] While A. G. Spalding & Bros. was not among the original six manufacturers, they eventually joined and published this standard color chart of athletic felt for consumer reference.

While some shades were universal, Spalding offered "special colors" only available through their brand. Athletic felt, typically a wool-blend fabric, was used for letters and numbers on sporting uniforms. At some point, this chart was annotated, possibly by a customer, expressing a preference for "No. 12 Kelley Green."

56

ATHLETIC GOODS MANUFACTURERS' ASSOCIATION

STANDARD COLOR CHART

The felt swatches shown in this folder represent the twenty basic standardized colors selected by the Athletic Goods Manufacturers' Association.

> When ordering Athletic Clothing be sure and specify standard color name and number to avoid confusion and error.

A. G. SPALDING & BROS.

Stores in All Leading Cities

ATHLETIC GOODS MANUFACTURERS' ASSOCIATION

Standard Color Chart
Instructions

1—The twenty all wool felt samples shown on this color card represent standard shades adopted and approved by the Athletic Goods Manufacturers' Association.

2—These shades are made with the best fast dyes known to chemists to produce fastness to light, perspiration, competent laundering, and salt water.

3—Every care is taken in manufacturing to insure a close match, but due to the peculiar characteristics of these dyes, it should be understood that some variation is necessary and allowable.

4—Dry cleaning is recommended for best results.

A. G. SPALDING & BROS.

Stores in All Leading Cities

Cats. 24–25

Patches from Hillsborough High School,
New Hampshire, 1920–30
Wool
4 × 3 × 0.1 cm (1 9/16 × 1 3/16 × 1/16 in.) and
2.1 × 4.5 × 0.1 cm (13/16 × 1 3/4 × 1/16 in.)
New Hampshire Historical Society,
2012.008.03.2 and 2012.008.03.3

These two twentieth-century patches
from Hillsborough High School baseball
uniforms demonstrate the material
process of adorning the jersey. Letters
would be cut from athletic felt and
then stitched onto the jerseys per the
customer's request. The rectangular
logo of the high school was sewn with
a running stitch to hold the letterforms
in place. White and burgundy felt
reflected the school's colors and added
an eye-catching flourish to an otherwise
standard uniform.

Cat. 23

Ray Fisher Postcard, 1911
Real photo postcard
14 × 8.9 cm (5 1/2 × 3 1/2 in.)
Bennington Museum, Museum
Purchase, 2019.15.83

On June 11, 1911, Bennington's
baseball team played against North
Adams from Massachusetts. The game
manager negotiated local Vermont
favorite Ray Fisher, who was playing for
New York at the time, to pitch against
North Adams.[8] By donning Bennington's
uniform, Fisher temporarily swapped his
identity. His button-down jersey has a
contrasting color for the button line, a
cadet-style collar, and a block letter *B* in
athletic felt.

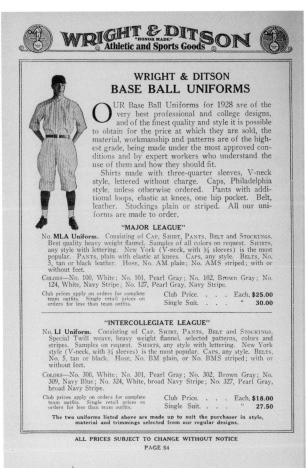

Cat. 26

Wright & Ditson
(American, founded 1871)
*Wright & Ditson Spring and Summer
Catalogue*, 1928
14 × 20.2 cm (5½ × 7¹⁵⁄₁₆ in.)
Historic New England

Founded in 1871 by Hall of Famer
George Wright and businessman Henry
Ditson, Wright & Ditson sought to
control some of the sporting goods
market dominated by A. G. Spalding.
In the 1880s, the company had a
complete athletic line from equipment
to uniforms. Despite attempts to ward
off a takeover, Spalding purchased
Wright & Ditson in 1891, but allowed
them to continue to sell their name-
brand wares. The Wright & Ditson
uniforms varied little from Spalding,
constructed of varying grades of flannel
and tailor-made to order.

Cat. 26b

Interior page of the 1928 Wright &
Ditson catalogue.

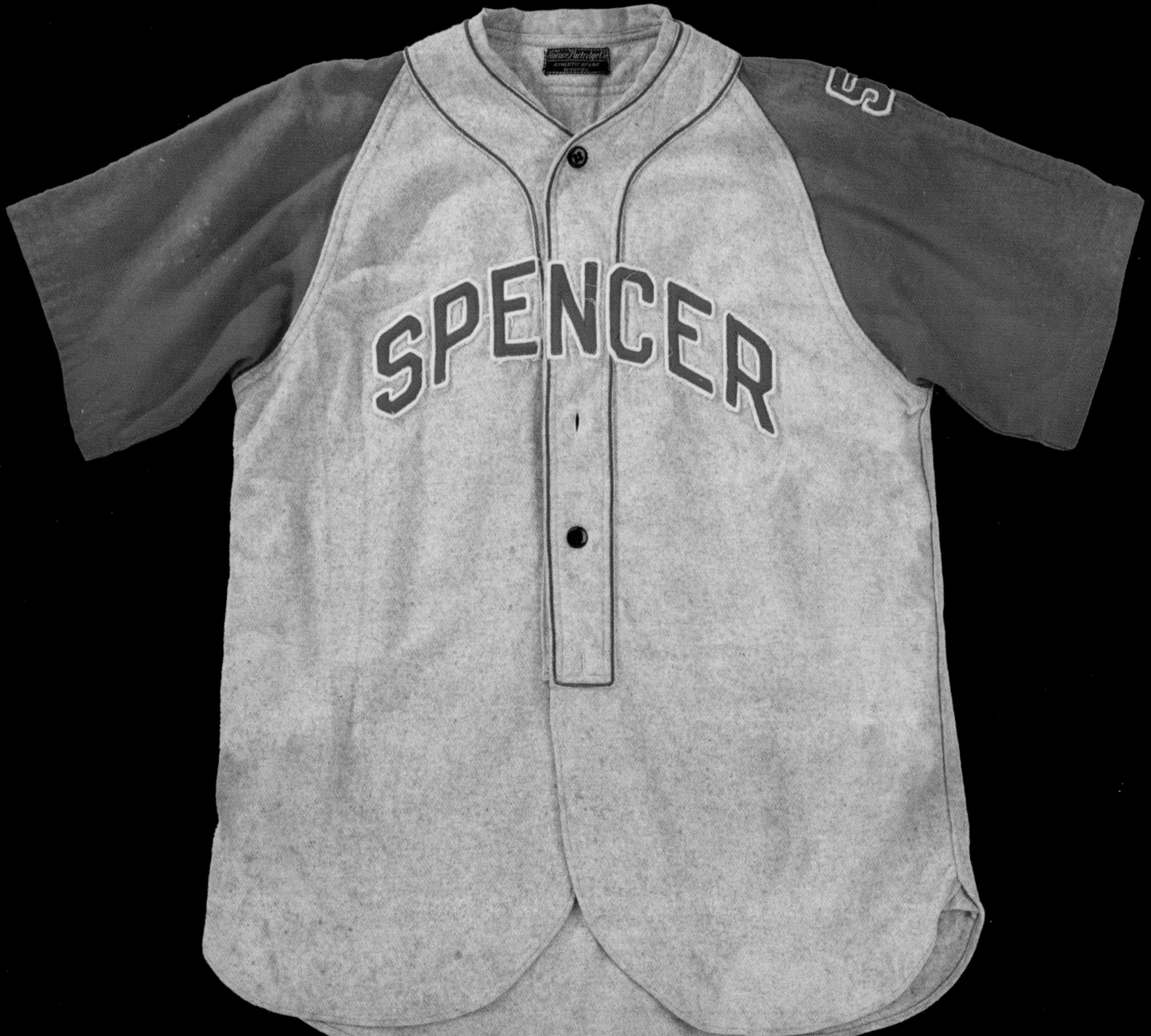
SPENCER
S

Cat. 27

Horace Partridge & Co.
(American, founded 1847)
Spencer Jersey, 1930s
Wool
83.8 × 88.9 cm (33 × 35 in.)
Courtesy of Central Mass
Auctions, Inc.

This colorful jersey worn by a local team from Spencer, Massachusetts, displays the modern jersey shape: short-sleeved, collarless, and button-down. To allow for a greater range of movement, manufacturers adopted the raglan sleeves, sometimes with contrasting colors, which have become a casual staple in contemporary fashion. Additional details are the matching trim around the button placket and block letters enhanced with another color of felt for visual contrast. Manufactured by the Boston company Horace Partridge & Co., this jersey represents the celebration of local ball.

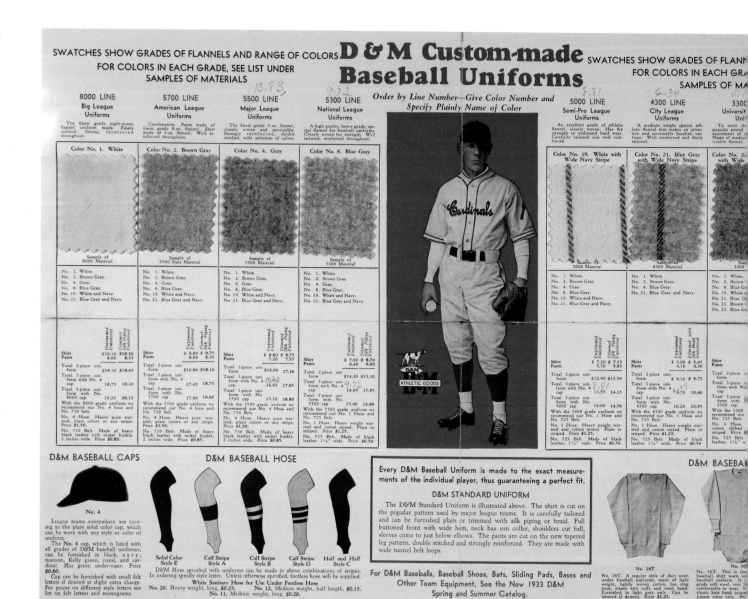

Cat. 28

Draper and Maynard
(American, 1840–1937)
Draper and Maynard
Company Booklet, 1933
Paper, textile, and wool
30.5 × 45.7 cm (12 × 18 in.)
New Hampshire Historical
Society, 2004.054

Draper and Maynard operated like many twentieth-century sporting goods manufacturers, with a network of dealers, traveling sales representatives, and mail-order catalogues. Customers would browse the biannual catalogue (usually divided by seasonal specific sports) and could inquire about a sample book of fabric options. This fabric swatch booklet presents material samples noting the colors and varying weights or quality of the flannel. An effective marketing tool, the swatch book enabled the customer to make an informed purchase by appealing to tactile and visual senses. Although each uniform was individually tailored, Draper and Maynard used a standard uniform pattern rather than stocking multiple types of shirt silhouettes.

O RANGE OF COLORS

LIST UNDER

**3000 LINE
Junior League
Uniforms**

A light weight, but strong and serviceable flannel. Well tailored and reinforced. Made on the same pattern as all D&M uniforms as illustrated.

Color No. 4. Gray

Sample of 3000 Material

No. 4. Gray.
No. 21. Blue Gray and Navy.

No. 3T. For the sweat shirt type of baseball uniform, the No. 3T is ideally adapted. It is silver gray in color, and makes a pleasing combination when used with a plain gray or gray with navy blue striped pant. Can be lettered and used in place of regular uniform shirt. See prices on felt letters and monograms. Price $1.00.

D&M CUSTOM MADE BASEBALL UNIFORMS

DRAPER-MAYNARD Custom Made Uniforms are recognized everywhere as the finest that can be produced both in quality of material and in superior workmanship. Each uniform is made in exact accordance with the measurements of the individual player. We guarantee D&M Custom Made Uniforms to fit perfectly. The flannels used are the best obtainable and our reinforced uniforms will stand the hard abuse of a league campaign.

In the D&M line of Custom Made baseball uniforms are ten different grades ranging all the way from "The Big League" Uniforms down to "Boys'" Uniforms. These are available in a wide assortment of colors, in plain and striped flannels.

The ten grades are as follows:

(Five pieces: Shirt, Pants, trimmed, unlettered, Cap, Belt, Hose)

The 8000 Line, Big League Uniforms $24.00
The 5700 Line, Am. League Uniforms $22.70
The 5500 Line, Major League Uniforms $21.45
The 5300 Line, Nat. League Uniforms $17.06
The 5000 Line, Ind. League Uniforms $15.58
The 4800 Line, Inter-Urban Leag. Uni. $14.76
The 4200 Line, College Leag. Uniforms $13.06
The 3300 Line, University Uniforms $10.41
The 3000 Line, Junior Leag. Uniforms $7.02
The 500 Line, Boys' Uni. (untrimmed) $5.00

Ask your dealer or write for the Special D&M Baseball Uniform Catalog, which contains samples of flannels, prices and convenient measurement blanks.

**Your Local D&M Dealer
is prepared to quote
SPECIAL PRICES
to Schools and Clubs**

• 26 •

Fig. 24. Interior page of the 1932 Spring and Summer Draper and Maynard catalogue, showing baseball uniforms.

Fig. 25. Draper and Maynard order form for sporting goods.

Fig. 26. A Draper and Maynard worker ironing baseball uniforms in the company's Plymouth, New Hampshire factory.

Cat. 29

Spalding (American, founded 1876)
Boston Red Sox Uniform Shirt, worn by
Robert Moses "Lefty" Grove, 1938
Wool flannel
106.7 × 89.5 cm (42 × 35¼ in.)
National Baseball Hall of Fame and
Museum, B-331-73

Unlike the 1938 Red Sox home whites
that displayed silk piping and fancy
lettering, this road uniform worn by
pitcher Robert Moses "Lefty" Grove
was notably plainer. The gray of the
Red Sox road uniforms is a traditional
color, dating back to the nineteenth
century when players wore darker-
hued uniforms on the road reputedly
to cover the dirt stains. Block capital
letters in navy athletic felt spell out the
team's city, BOSTON. Manufactured
by Spalding, the jersey features elastic
cotton-knit underarm gussets to
provide a greater range of motion, a
detail particularly noteworthy for a
pitcher's jersey.

Fig. 27. Leslie Jones, Lefty Grove of the
Sox with N.Y. Yankee, glass negative,
1938, Boston Public Library, Leslie
Jones Collection.

Robert Moses "Lefty" Grove in his Red
Sox home uniform with New York Yankee
pitcher Wes Ferrell in 1938.

Cat. 30

Koronis Sports Apparel, Inc.
Replica 1946 Boston Red Sox Jersey
Worn by Johnny Pesky, 2002
Wool
Courtesy of the Boston Red Sox

Throwback jerseys, often popular
marketing events, take on special
significance around team reunions or
ceremonies. Following Hall of Famer
Ted Williams's death, the Boston Red
Sox hosted a celebration of life at
Fenway Park. Former teammate Johnny
Pesky wore this replica 1946 jersey in
honor of Williams. In 1946 Williams
helped the Red Sox win the American
League pennant and received the MVP
(most valuable player) award, following
three years of military service during
World War II. By wearing a jersey from
one of Williams's most spectacular
years, Pesky and others paid tribute
to the "Splendid Splinter" and the
Red Sox community.

Fig. 28. Johnny Pesky at "Ted Williams: A
Celebration of an American Hero," Fenway
Park, July 22, 2002.

Cat. 31

Cleveland Buckeyes Shirt,
worn by Ernie Wright Jr., 1946–48
Wool
National Baseball Hall of Fame and
Museum, B-380-85

Ernie Wright—a Black entrepreneur
from Erie, Pennsylvania—founded the
Cleveland Buckeyes in the fall of 1941.[9]
The team's uniform bore the popular
mid-twentieth-century slanted script
with a flourish, inside which "Buckeyes"
is stitched in red thread. Like many
sports uniforms, this baseball jersey
draws inspiration from military uniforms
with dual colored piping and stripes
trimming the button placket and the
sleeves to enhance and convey strength
and power. A large patch on the left
sleeve indicates the Buckeyes' champion
status after winning the Negro League
World Series title in 1945.

Fig. 29. John W. Mosely, *1946 Cleveland
Buckeyes*, black and white photograph,
1946, the Charles L. Blockson Afro-
American Collection, Temple
University Libraries.

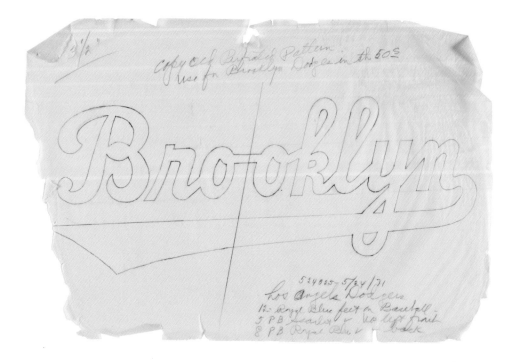

Cat. 32

R. J. Liebe Athletic Lettering Company
(American, founded 1923)
Brooklyn Dodgers Pattern, 1950s
Graphite on paper
29.8 × 44.5 cm (11¾ × 17½ in.)
Courtesy of the R. J. Liebe Athletic
Lettering Company

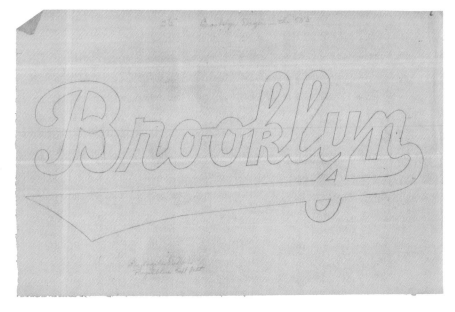

Cat. 33

R. J. Liebe Athletic Lettering Company
(American, founded 1923)
Brooklyn Dodgers Pattern, 1950s
Diazotype
27.9 × 43.2 cm (11 × 17 in.)
Courtesy of the R. J. Liebe Athletic
Lettering Company

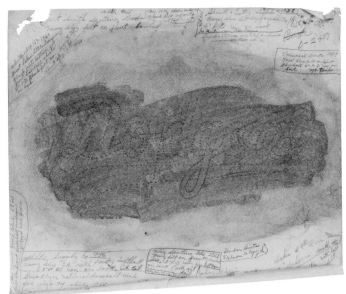

R. J. Liebe Athletic Lettering Company
(American, founded 1923)
Brooklyn Dodgers Pattern, 1950s
Ink and graphite on paper
36.8 × 44.1 cm (14½ × 17⅜ in.)
Courtesy of the R. J. Liebe Athletic
Lettering Company

Cat. 35

R. J. Liebe Athletic Lettering Company
(American, founded 1923)
Brooklyn Dodgers Stencil, 1950s
Ink and graphite on paper
37.5 × 44.8 cm (14¾ × 17⅝ in.)
Courtesy of the R. J. Liebe Athletic
Lettering Company

Founded by Robert Liebe and his wife in their Saint Louis basement, the R. J. Liebe Athletic Lettering Company has gone on to make the lettering, numbers, and patches for numerous Major League teams, including the St. Louis Cardinals. By the 1950s, the company was employing over sixty workers, many of whom were women. In the pre-digital era, all lettering was sewn by hand using paper stencils as guides. The lettering was drawn on tracing paper and then run through a blueprint machine to make copies for stencils. Unless requested by the teams, the lettering remained the same from year to year. These transparencies bear years' worth of annotations about color, placement, and scale.

Patterns were transferred to the felt through small holes on cardboard copies through a dauber dipped in blue paste mixed with gasoline. The fabric was stacked in ten to twelve layers and run by hand through a Liebe-designed machine to cut out the letters.[10]

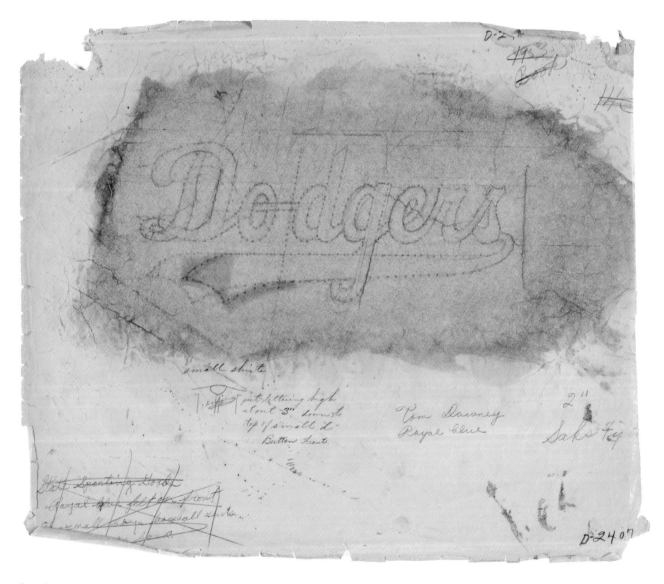

Cat. 36

R. J. Liebe Athletic Lettering Company
(American, founded 1923)
Brooklyn Dodgers Stencil, 1950s
Ink and graphite on paper
36.8 × 44.1 cm (14½ × 17⅜ in.)
Courtesy of the R. J. Liebe Athletic
Lettering Company

The R. J. Liebe Athletic Lettering
Company devised a means to achieve
a consistent aesthetic appearance
with jersey lettering that went over
the button placket, known as a "tuck
under." The diagonal line in the stencil
shows where the opening would be
on the jersey. Notably, there is an
elongated flourish between the o and

the d that would be tucked under
the button placket. This created a
seamless line when the button placket
gaped during a player's movement.
The stencil includes a small drawing to
indicate how the lettering would appear
on the jersey.

Cat. 37

R. J. Liebe Athletic Lettering Company
(American, founded 1923)
Brooklyn Dodgers Felt Sample, 1950s
Felt
21.6 × 46.4 cm (8½ × 18¼ in.)
Courtesy of the R. J. Liebe Athletic
Lettering Company

The blue and white lettering on this
Brooklyn Dodgers sample would have
been inlayed by hand. An inlayer would
apply an adhesive between the layers,
which was activated through a heat
press machine. One Liebe employee,
Betty Jones, was noted for her skill at
inlaying—a difficult task as it required
the employee to place the letters
without measuring. Once inlayed,
the fabric letters would be stitched
together on a sewing machine.

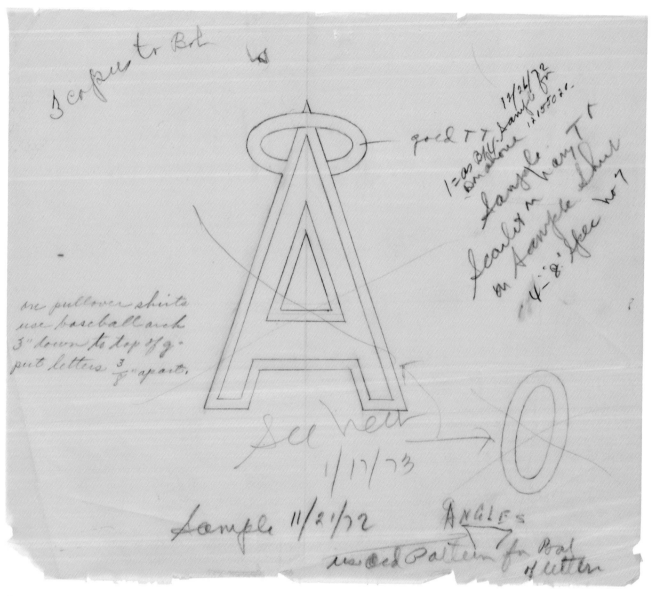

Cat. 38

R. J. Liebe Athletic Lettering Company
(American, founded 1923)
California Angels Pattern, 1972
Graphite on paper
4 × 43.2 cm (5½ × 17 in.)
Courtesy of the R. J. Liebe Athletic
Lettering Company

Cat. 39

R. J. Liebe Athletic Lettering Company
(American, founded 1923)
California Angels Pattern, 1972–73
Diazotype
24.4 × 28.3 cm (9⅝ × 11⅛ in.)
Courtesy of the R. J. Liebe Athletic
Lettering Company

R. J. Liebe Athletic Lettering Company's
paper patterns serve as a visual archive
of baseball logo modifications. For
their 1973 jerseys, the California
Angels asked to modify their lowercase
letters from 1972 to include a capital
A with a halo.

Cat. 40

R. J. Liebe Athletic Lettering Company
(American, founded 1923)
New York Yankees (verso), 1950s
Metal
14.3 × 14 × 1.9 cm (5⅝ × 5½ × ¾ in.)
Courtesy of the R. J. Liebe Athletic
Lettering Company

The New York Yankees are one of the
few teams that rarely changes their
lettering, evident in this comparison
of the iconic *NY* monogram over
fifty years. By the 1980s, the R. J.
Liebe Athletic Lettering Company
switched from cardboard stencils to
more durable metal dies. When heavy
weight was applied, the die would cut
through layers of fabric to produce the
lettering (Cat. 41).

Cat. 41

R. J. Liebe Athletic Lettering Company
(American, founded 1923)
New York Yankees, 1980s–90s
Fabric
14 × 14 cm (5½ × 5½ in.)
Courtesy of the R. J. Liebe Athletic
Lettering Company

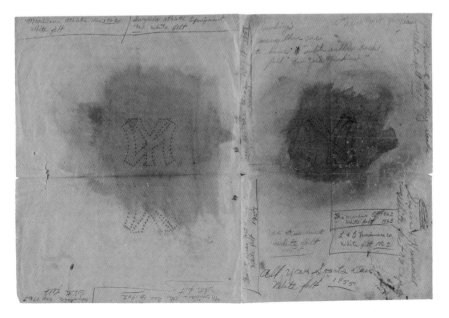

Cat. 42

R. J. Liebe Athletic Lettering Company
(American, founded 1923)
New York Yankees, around 1960s
Ink and graphite on paper
Open: 30.5 × 45.7 cm (12 × 18 in.)
Courtesy of the R. J. Liebe Athletic
Lettering Company

1960

SPRING &
SUMMER

Stall&Dean
ATHLETIC EQUIPMENT

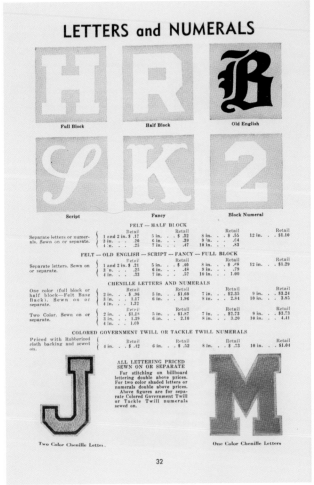

Cat. 43

Stall & Dean Sporting Goods Company (American, founded 1898)
Stall & Dean Athletic Equipment, Spring/Summer 1960
22.9 × 15.2 cm (9 × 6 in.)

Touted as the "world's largest uniform manufacturer," Stall & Dean captured a significant share of the twentieth-century uniform and apparel market.[11] In 1910 they debuted their "Safeslide" flannel line, a durable, preshrunk wool flannel with the color woven into the fabric rather than dyed. Their catalogue offered a range of monograms, letters, and numbers to adorn the uniforms, providing customers with an array of customization options.

Cat. 43b–c

Options for emblems, monograms, letters, and numbers to adorn jerseys and other sporting attire.

Cat. 44

Stall & Dean Sporting Goods Company
(American, founded 1898)
Baseball Jersey
Fabric
64 × 50 cm (25 3/16 × 19 11/16 in.)
Smithsonian National Museum of
American History, 1998.0324.55

Twentieth-century uniform and apparel
manufacturer Stall & Dean began
in Brockton, Massachusetts. While
manufacturers offered a range of adult
uniforms from professional to college,
many also created youth or junior
uniforms. Little League, founded in
1939, provided an organized, youth-
focused baseball club outside of school

teams. As the uniform reads "Stall &
Dean," in the place of a team name or
city, this was likely a display sample or a
company team jersey.

Cat. 46

McAuliffe Uniform Company
(American, founded 1969)
Milwaukee Brewers Jersey, worn by Hank Aaron, 1975
Cotton and nylon
88.9 × 81.3 cm (35 × 32 in.)
Smithsonian National Museum of American History, Gift of Milwaukee Brewers Baseball Club (through Thomas J. Ferguson), 1977.1133.01

Legendary ballplayer Hank Aaron wore this double knit Brewers pullover upon his return to Milwaukee in 1975. Bold blue and yellow striped elastic bands on the sleeves and collar not only add a bright pop of color, but also added comfort for the players. Distributed under the McAuliffe Uniform Company label, this jersey was actually manufactured by Brockton distributer Stall & Dean.[12] Aaron's number, 44, would be retired from the Brewers rotation the following year, communicating the importance of numerals in baseball and the identification of a player with his or her number.

Cat. 45

The Sporting News
(American, founded 1886)
The Dope Book, 1962
16.8 × 12.4 × 1 cm (6⅝ × 4⅞ × ⅜ in.)

An annual magazine published by the Sporting News, *The Dope Book* provided baseball fans with all the pertinent information or "dope" of the day. Rosters, schedules, statistics, and even park diagrams filled the pages. But the cover of the 1962 edition indicates a visual shift toward branded logos and mascots. Laid out in a modernist grid, all twenty MLB teams are represented by logos. Taking a cue from mid-twentieth-century advertising and the popularity of animation, many of the logos adopted cartoon or caricatured features, some of which have remained until the present day. This edition of *The Dope Book* depicts logos that would soon be altered, including the Houston Colts (renamed the Astros) and the Kansas City Athletics (moved to Oakland).

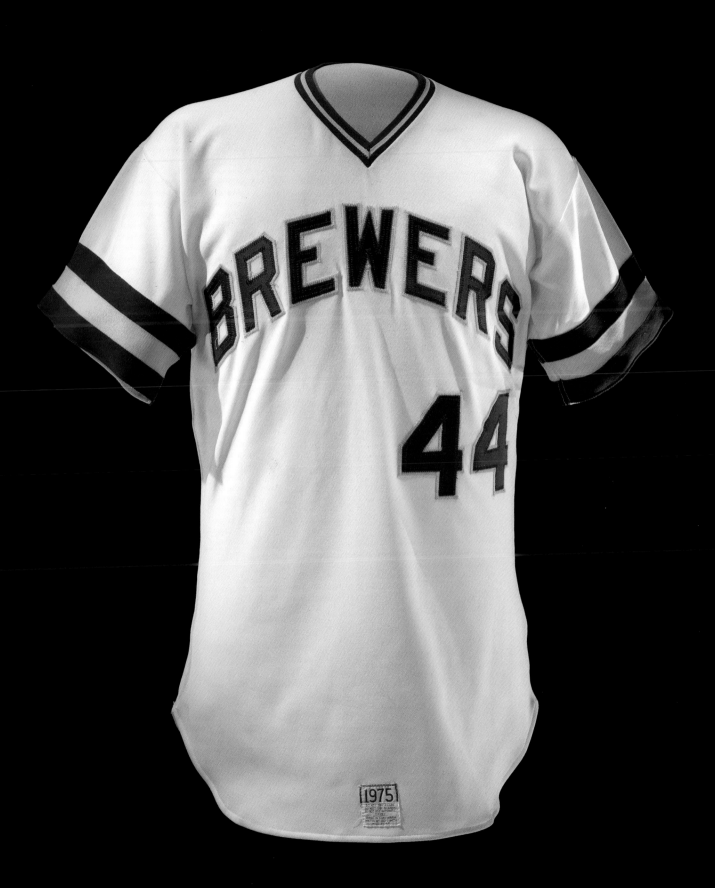

Cat. 47

Powers Manufacturing Company
(American, founded 1902)
Saint Vincent College Bearcats Uniform
Shirt, worn by Jodi Haller, about 1991
Double knit (polyester)
71.1 × 47.6 cm (28 × 18¾ in.)
National Baseball Hall of Fame and
Museum, B-252-2018

Most baseball teams are segregated
by gender with women playing softball
over baseball. Jodi Haller, however,
disagreed with the gender division,
stating: "I've never even considered
playing softball. I like the challenge of
baseball."[13] She became the first woman
to pitch in a college game and the third
ever to play college ball. Her uniform
is a double knit pullover with the 1930s
slanted script with a flourish. Also
indicative of the period are the racing
stripes on the sleeves, a design feature
that modernized the uniform with a
streamlined appearance.

Fig. 30. Jodi Haller with the
Saint Vincent College men's
baseball team.

Cat. 48

Todd Radom (American, b. 1964)
Milwaukee Pencil Lettering, 1993
Pencil on paper
27.9 × 43.2 cm (11 × 17 in.)
Courtesy of the artist

Cat. 49

Todd Radom (American, b. 1964)
Milwaukee Ink Lettering, 1993
Pencil on paper
27.9 × 43.2 cm (11 × 17 in.)
Courtesy of the artist

Cat. 50

Todd Radom (American, b. 1964)
Brewers Lettering, 1993
India ink on tracing paper,
spray-mounted to paper
27.9 × 43.2 cm (11 × 17 in.)
Courtesy of the artist

A graphic designer specializing in sports logos and branding, Todd Radom created the letterforms for the 1994 Milwaukee Brewers jerseys. After refining a series of letters on tracing paper, Radom finalizes the sketches using technical drawing tools to perfect the design. The artwork is then inked with a radiograph pen on Denril paper, a specialty multimedia vellum used for drafting. To transfer the final designs onto the jersey, Radom takes a photostat, a type of black-and-white photocopy ideal for reproducing artwork, and sends the copy to the jersey manufacturer. The photostat serves as the source image as the manufacturer cuts letters out of twill or vinyl to be sewn onto the jersey.

MAJOR LEAGUE BASEBALL TEAMS
AND THEIR PANTONE® COLORS

ALL PRIMARY CLUB COLORS

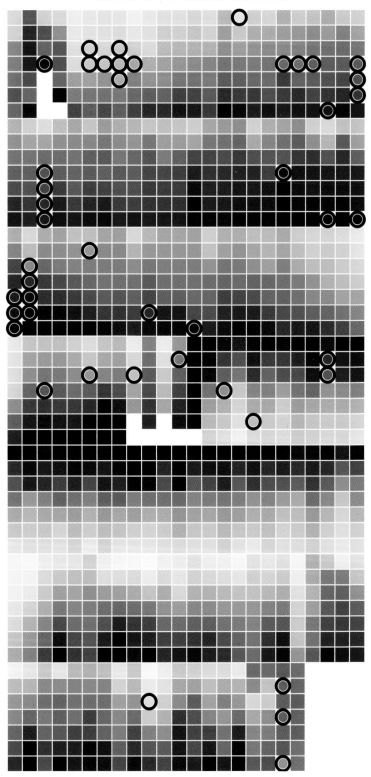

Cat. 51

Craig Robinson (British, active Mexico)
Major League Baseball Teams and Their
Pantone Colors, 2012
Courtesy of the artist

Graphic designer Craig Robinson
produced an enlightening infographic
about MLB and their Pantone colors.
The breakdown of teams' colors shows
clusters around black, red, navy blue,
and gray, traditional colors originating
from historic flannels. Notably, teams
tend to name their colors after their
nicknames—for instance, Cubbie blue
or Dodgers blue—but these are actually
the same Pantone color (294). There
are also significant outliers, such as
Seattle's hunter green (329), Arizona's
tawny beige (7501), and Tampa Bay's
light blue (292).

EACH TEAM'S COLORS

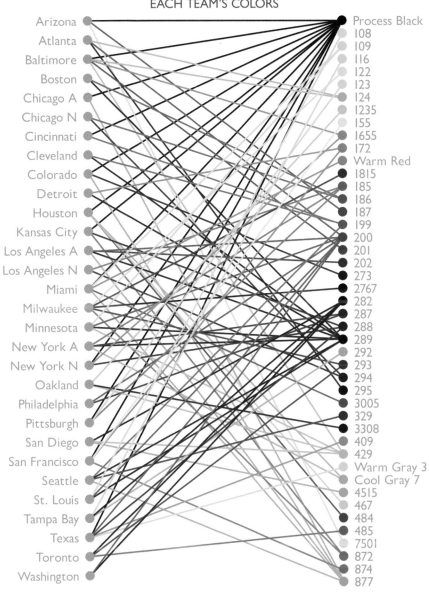

Teams	Colors
Arizona	Process Black
Atlanta	108
Baltimore	109
Boston	116
Chicago A	122
Chicago N	123
Cincinnati	124
Cleveland	1235
Colorado	155
Detroit	1655
Houston	172
Kansas City	Warm Red
Los Angeles A	1815
Los Angeles N	185
Miami	186
Milwaukee	187
Minnesota	199
New York A	200
New York N	201
Oakland	202
Philadelphia	273
Pittsburgh	2767
San Diego	282
San Francisco	287
Seattle	288
St. Louis	289
Tampa Bay	292
Texas	293
Toronto	294
Washington	295
	3005
	329
	3308
	409
	429
	Warm Gray 3
	Cool Gray 7
	4515
	467
	484
	485
	7501
	872
	874
	877

MOST COMMONLY USED COLORS

Pantone Process Black ARI BAL CIN COL CWS HOU KC MIA NYM PIT SF TEX

Pantone 289 BOS CLE DET LAA MIN NYY SEA STL

Pantone 200 ATL LAA MIN PHI STL TEX WSH

Pantone 877 COL CWS LAA MIA SEA

Pantone 282 SD TB TOR WSH

Pantone 429 BAL MIN OAK SD

Cat. 52

Brian Finke (American, b. 1976)
Royals, 2013
C-type print
76.2 × 76.2 cm (30 × 30 in.)
Courtesy of the artist and
ClampArt, New York City

Photographer Brian Finke documented
the process of making baseball cards
through his 2013 *Topps* series. Taken
during the annual picture day of spring
training, players pose for photographs
that will be used in publications
and baseball cards. In an era before
television, baseball cards served as the
primary visual medium for introducing
what players and their uniforms looked
like to fans. The tradition continues
even in today's visually saturated age.
Simply titled *Royals*, Finke's photograph
demonstrates the importance of the
jersey in visual culture through its
reproduction and dissemination in
baseball cards.

Cat. 53

Tabitha Soren (American, b. 1967)
Matt Flemer, Modesto Nuts, 2014
Unique tintype
32.4 × 27.3 cm (12¾ × 10¾ in.)
Courtesy of the artist

Cat. 54

Tabitha Soren (American, b. 1967)
Ryon Healy, Stockton Ports (now Milwaukee Brewers), 2014
Unique tintype
27.3 × 32.4 cm (10¾ × 12¾ in.)
Courtesy of the artist

Cat. 55

Tabitha Soren (American, b. 1967)
Marco Scutaro, San Francisco Giants, 2014
Unique tintype
32.4 × 27.3 cm (12¾ × 10¾ in.)
Courtesy of the artist

Cat. 56

Tabitha Soren (American, b. 1967)
Lonnie Chisenhall, Cleveland Indians, 2013
Unique tintype
32.4 × 27.3 cm (12¾ × 10¾ in.)
Courtesy of the artist

Cat. 58

Tabitha Soren (American, b. 1967)
Carl Yastrzemski, Red Sox, 2014
Unique tintype
27.3 × 32.4 cm (10¾ × 12¾ in.)
Courtesy of the artist

Cat. 57

Tabitha Soren (American, b. 1967)
Tim Alderson, Stockton Ports, 2015
Unique tintype
32.4 × 27.3 cm (12¾ × 10¾ in.)
Courtesy of the artist

Cat. 59

Tabitha Soren (American, b. 1967)
Sam Fuld, Oakland A's, 2014
Unique tintype
27.3 × 32.4 cm (10¾ × 12¾ in.)
Courtesy of the artist

Cat. 60

Tabitha Soren (American, b. 1967)
World Series Ring, Red Sox, 2013
Unique tintype
27.3 × 32.4 cm (10¾ × 12¾ in.)
Courtesy of the artist

Tabitha Soren's *Fantasy Life* series began as a documentation of the Oakland A's rookie class in 2002, but ultimately grew into a twelve-year project capturing the career highlights and lowlights of twenty-one hopeful players.[14] As the series moved beyond the original players, Soren began to chronicle moments of success and failure with more well-known players. Using the tintype medium that was invented during baseball's infancy, Soren creates nostalgic work firmly rooted in the present. A slow-exposure medium, tintypes are typically ill-suited for the action shots of sports photography, but after much trial and error Soren developed a method to capture motion. Her photographs reveal the prominence of graphic design in the players' uniforms.

Cat. 61

Majestic Athletic
(American, founded 1976)
Boston Strong Jersey, 2013
Polyester
Courtesy of the Boston Red Sox

Following the Boston Marathon
bombing on April 15, 2013, Boston
Red Sox player David Ortiz announced
during pregame ceremonies: "This
jersey we are wearing today, it doesn't
say, 'Red Sox,' it says, 'Boston.'"[15] Rather
than wear their traditional "Red Sox"
jerseys, the team would wear home
whites with "Boston" across the chest,
usually reserved for their away jerseys.
The name change and the "B Strong"
patch placed over the heart helped
to unify and promote healing for a
community dealing with the trauma of
terrorism. Due to the overwhelming
support for the jerseys, the Red Sox
now don their "Boston Strong" jerseys
every Patriots' Day to memorialize and
reflect on the tragic event.

Fig. 31. David Ortiz speaking during
pregame ceremonies on April 20, 2013.

Fig. 32. Worcester Red Sox jersey
advertisement for their inaugural season.

Cat. 62

Majestic Athletic
(American, founded 1976)
Worcester Red Sox Jersey
Polyester
Courtesy of the Worcester Red Sox

When the Triple-A affiliate of the
Boston Red Sox announced they would
be moving from Pawtucket, Rhode
Island to Worcester, Massachusetts the
team needed new jerseys. The first of
nine jersey designs for the Worcester
Red Sox's inaugural 2021 season, this
traditional white button-down with
"Worcester" in red across the front
draws inspiration from their MLB team.
The white jersey with red piping around
the button placket are the same on
both the Boston and Worcester Red
Sox jerseys. But what visually connects
the two teams' jerseys, thereby
demonstrating an affiliation, is the
lettering that instantly reads as Red Sox.

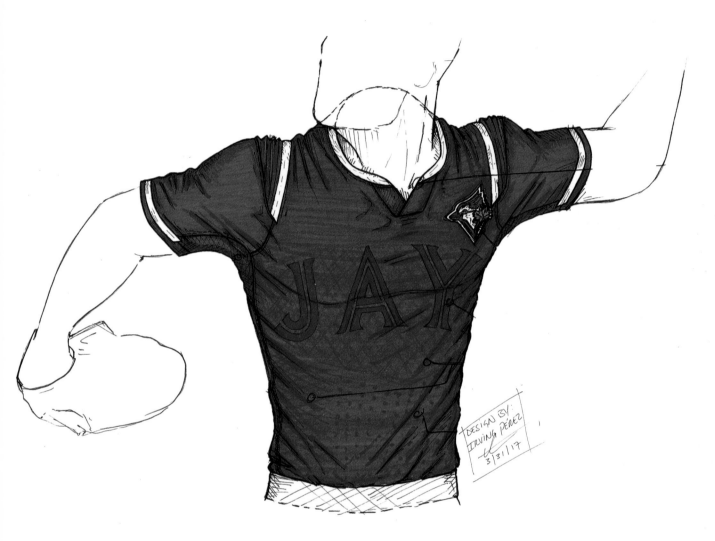

Cat. 63

Irving Perez (Mexican and American)
Proposed Design for Toronto Blue
Jays Jersey, 2017
Pencil, pen, and Copic marker on paper
27.9 × 43.2 cm (11 × 17 in.)
Courtesy of the artist

Today's baseball jersey, despite the high-tech fabrics, still resembles the oversize flannel of the 1930s. After studying the movements of players and their variable environments, sportswear designer Irving Perez reconceived the baseball jersey. He developed a new jersey reminiscent of the 1970s pullover, but in a slimmer cut, made of cutting-edge fabrics and including details such as 3D printed logos and bonding tape on the sleeves, all designed to enhance performance.

Cat. 64

Irving Perez (Mexican and American)
Fuji Uniform, 2017
Jersey: Engineered knit stretch
polyester (92 percent poly, 8 percent
Lycra); Pants: Knit polyester (98
percent poly, 2 percent Lycra) and
stretch polyester (92 percent poly, 8
percent Lycra)
Courtesy of the artist

As a student in the prestigious sports product design program at the University of Oregon, Irving Perez gave the baseball uniform a complete overhaul for the twenty-first century. Using Portland as his inspiration, Perez acknowledged baseball's racist history of segregation and named his fictional team after the city's Japanese American ball club, Fuji Athletic Club. Formed in 1927, the

Fuji Athletic Club became part of a West Coast network of baseball teams and fostered international relations with Japan. The club disbanded as a result of the forced incarceration of Japanese Americans during World War II. In understanding this legacy of oppression and endurance, Perez seeks to "revitalize the culture of the sport and ignite innovative thought for the baseball uniform."[16]

Figs. 33–35. Players testing the Fuji uniform on the field.

Fig. 36. Fuji uniform color scheme.

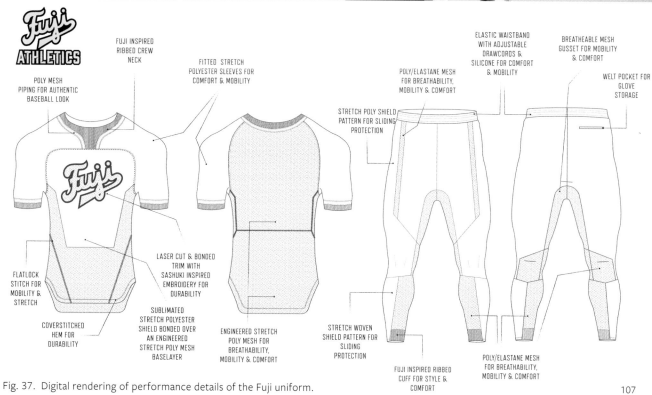

POLY MESH
PIPING FOR AUTHENTIC
BASEBALL LOOK

FUJI INSPIRED
RIBBED CREW
NECK

FITTED STRETCH
POLYESTER SLEEVES FOR
COMFORT & MOBILITY

ELASTIC WAISTBAND
WITH ADJUSTABLE
DRAWCORDS &
SILICONE FOR COMFORT
& MOBILITY

BREATHEABLE MESH
GUSSET FOR MOBILITY
& COMFORT

POLY/ELASTANE MESH
FOR BREATHABILITY,
MOBILITY & COMFORT

WELT POCKET FOR
GLOVE
STORAGE

STRETCH POLY SHIELD
PATTERN FOR SLIDING
PROTECTION

FLATLOCK
STITCH FOR
MOBILITY &
STRETCH

LASER CUT & BONDED
TRIM WITH
SASHUKI INSPIRED
EMBROIDERY FOR
DURABILITY

COVERSTITCHED
HEM FOR
DURABILITY

SUBLIMATED
STRETCH POLYESTER
SHIELD BONDED OVER
AN ENGINEERED
STRETCH POLY MESH
BASELAYER

ENGINEERED STRETCH
POLY MESH FOR
BREATHABILITY,
MOBILITY & COMFORT

STRETCH WOVEN
SHIELD PATTERN FOR
SLIDING
PROTECTION

FUJI INSPIRED RIBBED
CUFF FOR STYLE &
COMFORT

POLY/ELASTANE MESH
FOR BREATHABILITY,
MOBILITY & COMFORT

Fig. 37. Digital rendering of performance details of the Fuji uniform.

EXPERIMENTAL DESIGN

For the American imagination, the classic button-down jersey is part of the nostalgia of baseball. It can, however, appear a bit conservative in comparison to uniforms worn by teams looking to buck tradition and reinvent the ballpark basic. Who can forget the stunning iconoclastic designs from the double knit era when the Houston Astros donned tequila sunrises, the Baltimore Orioles looked like candy corn, and the San Diego Padres' fans saw the inspirational heft of the taco in their team's new uniform? But it is not only the 1970s and 1980s that eschewed the traditional jersey.[1] Maverick jersey choices have existed throughout baseball's 170-year history, from satin jerseys that looked like pajamas to sleeveless shirts resembling "unfinished coats."[2] These jersey designs embraced new fabrics, colors, and shapes, challenging the perceived purity of baseball's iconic garment. Some modifications were practical, like vests and zippers, or provided greater mobility and efficiency—yet because they altered tradition, they were ultimately abandoned. Others were the questionable fancies of a marketing team or owner (1976 Chicago White Sox leisure suits, for instance), or a decision to enforce the gender divide. Are these instances the result of truly bad aesthetic choices, that is to say poor selections in fabric or shape, or do they merely deviate from tradition in a sport where its legacy and history are deeply revered? Fashion is subjective, even in baseball, and what was once "ugly" is now enjoying a renaissance.[3] As *USA Today* once noted: "That's the thing about sports jerseys: even the ugly ones were once *someone's* childhood obsession."[4]

The nineteenth century featured its share of peculiar design choices. After sporting goods magnate A. G. Spalding became the official supplier of the National League's baseballs, mitts, and uniforms, he used his influence in 1882 to enact a sartorial rainbow on the field. On opening day, teams in the National League debuted a startling kaleidoscope of colors as each position wore a uniform in a different color, an experimental scheme thought to make it easier for player identification, but having the opposite effect.[5] Players and fans shunned the lack of uniformity, referring to the new attire as "clown suits" and "zebra uniforms."[6] Confusion abounded on the field and off. The new dress code lasted only two months before the National League reverted to their original uniforms.

Silky satin uniforms made an appearance in the 1940s with the proliferation of night games.[7] As ballparks began to install electric lighting systems, franchises wanted to improve visibility for fans and players alike.

Fig. 38. Graphics designed by Todd Radom for his 2018 book, *Winning Ugly: A Visual History of the Most Bizarre Uniforms Ever Worn*.

Enter satin fabrics as a clever solution to enhancing the reflection of the light in a dazzling show. First debuted by the Brooklyn Dodgers in 1944, satin uniforms were soon adopted by the St. Louis Cardinals, Cincinnati Reds, and Boston Braves. Panned as "monkey suits" and "Little Lord Fauntleroy" uniforms, the satin jerseys were often derided as "the ladies' influence," based on claims that women's baseball inspired such a fabric change.[8] This sexist charge seems to be an unfounded exaggeration. The women players in the All-American Girls Professional Baseball League did wear uniforms that emphasized their femininity at the request of the teams' owners—one-piece, short-skirted tunics—but the only satin in their uniforms were the shorts. The male team uniforms required many more bolts of satin than their female counterparts. Ultimately, the satin uniforms proved uncomfortable during hot summer evenings and were deemed too impractical.[9]

But the "golden age of ugly uniforms" spans the 1970s through the 1990s.[10] New synthetic fabrics, also known as double knits, allowed sportswear designers the rare opportunity to reconceive the jersey. Opting for a formfitting pullover style, designers embraced blocks of vibrant colors made possible through synthetic fabrics; oversize, wraparound shapes; and contemporary, sans serif typography. As the manager of the Atlanta Braves said: "Mod's the word these days as far as baseball players are concerned."[11] This was the era of kelly green and bright gold, of head-to-toe powder blue, and of gradient rainbows, all colors and patterns well suited to color television. One sportswriter asked: "Can it be baseball when it's played in baby blue uniforms? Yellow uniforms? In blouses? In purple shoes?"[12] His incredulity implied a lack of support for baseball's updated look. As baseball jersey design has reverted to a more traditional shape and style in the twenty-first century, double knit throwback jerseys have seen a comeback among the fan base—a reminder that good design is subjective, if not cyclical.

While many Major League Baseball (MLB) teams in the late 1990s began to don throwback uniforms for "Turn Back the Clock" nights—a league-wide initiative that sought to capitalize on fan nostalgia—the Seattle Mariners opted for another approach altogether: futuristic uniforms dubbed "Turn Ahead the Clock." Devised as a marketing promotion, "Turn Ahead the Clock" jerseys explored what uniform design would look like in 2027, the team's fiftieth anniversary. Worn for a single game on July 18, 1998, the "Turn Ahead the Clock" jerseys featured a baggy, sleeveless design; enlarged logos; and new "techy" colors of metallic silver and maroon.[13] Due to the popularity of the Mariners' event, the MLB invited teams the following year to participate in a league-wide "Turn Ahead the Clock" event sponsored by Century 21 real estate. Rather than start anew, many of the 1999 jerseys adapted the Mariners' original design with a sleeveless shape and "logos so big you could read them from the cheap seats."[14] The over-the-top promotion led to backlash, with players mocking the "gaudy" getups as a "perfect pair of pajamas."[15] Whereas vintage throwbacks have become a marketing staple in the MLB, only the Mariners have resurrected the "Turn Ahead the Clock" gambit.[16]

Fans, as it seems, have a lot to say about baseball uniforms, spawning blogs and social media posts about the best and worst dressed teams. But a look at these lists reveals a limited consensus as to what is actually "good" or "bad," with some jerseys making it on both lists, such as the Houston Astros' rainbows. Clearly, there is no definitive answer. In a sport where tradition reigns supreme, change is generally perceived negatively. Adoration of the modern jersey abounds. But fashion is ever-changing, and what was once the subject of sartorial tirades is now garnering newfound respect and popularity. Without experimentation, the baseball jersey would remain stagnant, stuck in a nostalgic reprise, as contemporary sportswear designers lament. Jersey redesign has the potential to yield systematic change in baseball uniforms, propelling the nineteenth-century sport into the future. What will the baseball jersey of tomorrow look like?

NATIONAL BASE BALL
OFFICIAL
LEAGUE SCHEDULE,
—AND—
1882 ❖ GAME RECORD ❖ 1882

H. R. CUMMINGS, Publisher,
WORCESTER, - MASS.

P. O. Box 896.

Entered according to Act of Congress in the year 1881, by H. R. CUMMINGS, in the Office of the Librarian of Congress, at Washington.

LEAGUE UNIFORM.

Shirts,

Catcher—*Scarlet.*

First Base—*Scarlet and White.*   Pitcher—*Light Blue.*   Third Base—*Gray and White.*

Second Base—*Orange and Black.*   Short Stop—*Maroon.*

Right Field—*Gray.*   Center Field—*Red and Black.*   Left Field—*White.*

First Sub.—*Green.*   Second Sub.—*Brown.*

Pants, White; Belts, same as Shirt; Tie, White; Caps, square top, color same as Shirt; Shoes, Leather.

Club Colors.
STOCKINGS.

Boston, Red; Buffalo, Gray; Chicago, White; Cleveland, Navy Blue; Detroit, Old Gold; Troy, Green; Providence, Light Blue; Worcester, Brown.

Cat. 65

Published by H. R.
Cummings (American)
National Baseball Official League
Schedule and Game Record, 1882
Closed: 5.7 × 11.4 cm (2¼ × 4½ in.)
Courtesy of Central Mass Auctions, Inc.

A. G. Spalding persuaded the National
League to bring about a new system of
colorful uniforms in 1882. He helped
pass a rule that players' positions would
be identified by color-coded uniforms.
For instance, the first baseman would
wear scarlet and white, while the
second baseman would be outfitted in
orange and black. Only the stockings
would reflect each team's color.
Unsurprisingly, the cacophonous color
clashing led to disorientation on the
field and the league abandoned the
uniforms. This 1882 score book and
schedule provided fans with a textual
guide to distinguish the positions on the
field and each ball club.

Fig. 39. A cabinet card depicting
the 1882 Detroit Wolverines in their
multicolored jerseys.

Fig. 40. The 1882 Chicago White Stockings
in their multicolored uniforms, from
Harper's Weekly, October 14, 1882.

Cat. 66

Horace Partridge & Co.
(American, founded 1847)
Boston Braves Satin Jersey,
worn by Ray Martin, 1948
Satin
National Baseball Hall of Fame and
Museum, B-273-72

As artificial lighting was constructed
in ballparks for nighttime games, some
teams experimented with satin fabrics
for their uniforms to enhance visibility.
The Boston Braves debuted their satin
suits on May 11, 1946, in conjunction
with their first evening game.[1] The
dazzling sight of the new uniforms
prompted one editorial comment: "We'll
bet Abner Doubleday would get a real
boot out of a look at one of these gaudy
night contests, which have sprung
from the game he invented long, long
ago."[2] Designed for use only during
evening play, satin uniforms caught
and reflected the lights in a spectacle
of illumination on the field. Yet these
slinky uniforms were met with critical
disdain as gaudy and players complained
that they retained heat, making them
uncomfortable. The Braves only
wore their satin jerseys from 1946 to
1948, making this short-lived trend a
flash in the pan.

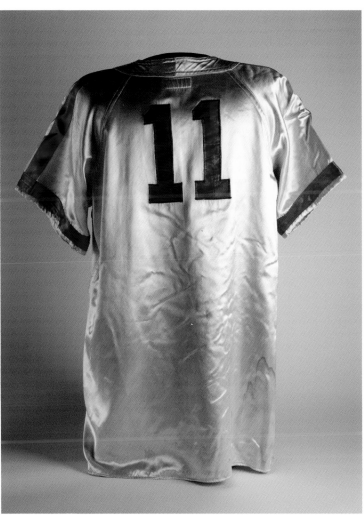

Fig. 41. Leslie Jones, Braves, glass negative,
ca. 1946–47, Boston Public Library, Leslie
Jones Collection.

Boston Braves' Nanny Fernandez, Mike
McCormick, and Danny Litwhiler wearing
their satin uniforms.

Cat. 67

Published by General Electric Company
(American, founded 1892)
The Magazine of Light, Volume 15,
Number 1, 1946
21.3 × 30.2 cm (8 ⅜ × 11 ⅞ in.)
Historic New England

The General Electric Company featured
the new artificial lights at Braves Field
on its magazine cover.

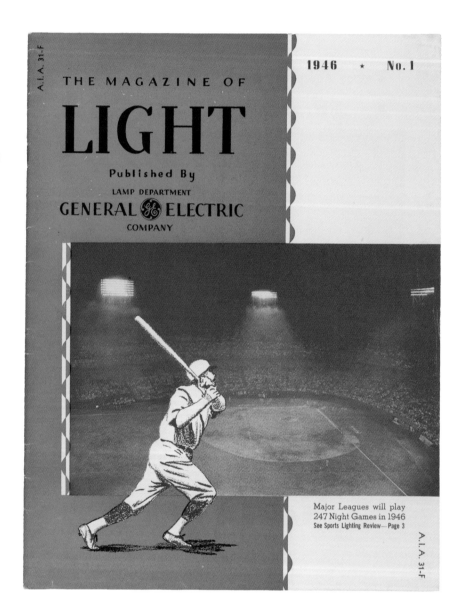

Braves Field—Home of the Boston Braves, Boston, Mass.   6

78547

Cat. 68

Tichnor Brothers (American, 1907–87)
Boston Braves Field—Home of the
Boston Braves, ca. 1930–45
Color postcard with linen texture
1.4 × 2.2 cm (3½ × 5½ in.)
Private collection

An aerial view postcard of Braves Field
lit up for a nighttime baseball game.

Cat. 69

King Sportswear Company (American)
Kalamazoo Lassies Uniform, worn by
Isabel "Lefty" Álvarez, ca. 1950s
Cotton
Courtesy of the International Women's
Baseball Center, Inc.

In 1943 Helen Wrigley, Otis Shepard,
and Chicago softball star Ann Harnett
collaborated to create uniforms for the
new All-American Girls Professional
Baseball League. Unlike men's baseball
attire of a jersey and pants, the women
donned one-piece, short-skirted tunics
made from cotton twill in a variety of
pastel hues. Designed to emphasize
the players' "feminine" qualities, the
uniforms' extra fabric and exposed
legs were impractical for baseball.
Doris "Sammye" Sams declared,
"Believe me, you haven't lived until
you've slid in skin," and Lois Youngen
said, "If you look at the uniform it's
got like three yards of material in it....
Have you ever tried to catch with your
arms and your dress goes up in the
air?"[3] The complications of playing
in such uniforms are an example of
how women's sportswear is often
gendered, reiterating stereotypes
of femininity rather than enhancing
performance. Isabel "Lefty" Álvarez,
a Cuban ballplayer who came to the
United States to play baseball, wore
this uniform while playing for the
Kalamazoo Lassies.

Fig. 42. G.W. Pach, Vassar College
baseball team: The Resolutes, 1876,
albumen print, Vassar College, Archives
and Special Collections, 08.17.

Even in the nineteenth century,
women's baseball uniforms reflected
traditional gender roles, as seen in the
Resolutes, Vassar College's baseball
team, in 1876.

Fig. 43. Women workers at the Rawlings uniform factory where Stan Musial's jersey would have been made.

Cat. 70

Rawlings (American, founded 1880s)
St. Louis Cardinals Jersey, worn by
Stan Musial, 1952
Cotton and metal
91.4 × 86.4 cm (36 × 34 in.)
Smithsonian National Museum of
American History, 2017.0084.11

An exemplar of the circular chain stitch, or a series of looped stitches, the St. Louis Cardinals' jerseys demonstrate the superior craftsmanship of the R. J. Liebe Athletic Lettering Company.[4] Starting in 1939, the Cardinals experimented with new jersey closures, moving away from buttons to the zipper. In the mid-twentieth century, the zipper industry promoted the novel fastener as acceptable in most clothing construction, including sporting attire.[5] Quick and efficient, the zipper became a design staple in mid-twentieth-century jerseys, even on the All-American Girls Professional Baseball League's tunics. But the fastener also awkwardly divides the embroidery and leaves long shirttails that necessitate the top be carefully tucked into the pants. The Cardinals abandoned the zipper for traditional buttons in 1956, but only after a seventeen-year run.

Cat. 71

Rawlings (American, founded 1880s)
Pittsburgh Pirates Uniform Vest, 1957
Polyester
87 × 52.1 cm (34¼ × 20½ in.)
National Baseball Hall of Fame and
Museum, B-256-2018

For the 1957–58 season, the Pittsburgh
Pirates debuted "a new look"—a
sleeveless shirt.[6] Designed to "give
greater freedom in fielding and batting,"
the vest was worn over a black shirt.
The vest modernized the overall
uniform appearance and decorative
details of black and gold piping around
the armholes and collar accentuated the
new style. Yet the sleeveless shirt was
essentially an extra uniform layer, with
players still wearing an undershirt—a
style used by the MLB today. While
other MLB teams experimented with
sleeveless shirts in the mid-twentieth
century, the Pirates wore the style for
fourteen years. It became one of their
signature looks until 1970, when they
introduced pullover jerseys to the MLB
for the first time.

1957

50¢

PITTSBURGH

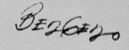

PIRATES

Cat. 72

Pittsburgh Pirates Yearbook, 1957
26.7 × 21.6 cm (10½ × 8½ in.)

The 1957 *Pittsburgh Pirates Yearbook* featured the team's new uniforms.

The "New Look" Continues in Pirates 1957 Uniforms

The "new look" in the Pirates started in 1956 under a new General Manager, Joe L. Brown, and a new field manager, Bobby Bragan. It continues this season in the form of new uniforms.

The main difference is in the uniform shirt, which is sleeveless, to give greater freedom in fielding and batting. The collar and arm holes are edged with black on gold piping. The shirt itself is white with "PIRATES" in black block letters with gold edging arched across the shirt front. Black numbers with gold edging are on the shirt back. The sweatshirts are black.

Trousers will be the same as last season with black on gold piping down the side.

The new uniforms are made from a light-weight flannel and dacron blend.

Socks are more colorful than last season's. The usual black socks have been brightened with three half-inch gold stripes at the top.

Pirates protective caps are of fiberglass, black with a gold block letter "P."

The road uniforms are the same as the home, except they are gray.

* new uniform is shown here modeled by Dick Groat, Pirate team captain and shortstop.

Fig. 44. Roberto Clemente, ca. 1957–69, National Baseball Hall of Fame and Museum, BL-4265-69.

Noted Pittsburgh Pirates player Roberto Clemente donning a sleeveless jersey.

Cat. 73

Walter Iooss Jr. (American, b. 1943)
*Tony Scott and Garry Templeton,
Dodger Stadium, Los Angeles*, 1979
Archival pigment print
50.8 × 61 cm (20 × 24 in.)
Penn Art Gallery, University of
Pennsylvania, 2015.0003.0001

Longtime *Sports Illustrated*
photographer Walter Iooss Jr. captured
some of the most iconic depictions of
the vibrant double knit era. Indicative
of the period's predilection for vivid
Technicolor, the St. Louis Cardinals cast
aside their traditional road grays for a
bright "victory blue" pullover. In 1978
Iooss walked into Dodger Stadium and
noticed the way the light emphasized
the blue walls. The following year, when
the Cardinals were scheduled to play
in Los Angeles, he knew that the blue
uniforms and red lettering against the
color of the ballpark would make for
a great picture.[7] Iooss said that the
photograph "had nothing to do with
the Cardinals, but the color of that
uniform and the color of the dugout in
Dodger Stadium."[8]

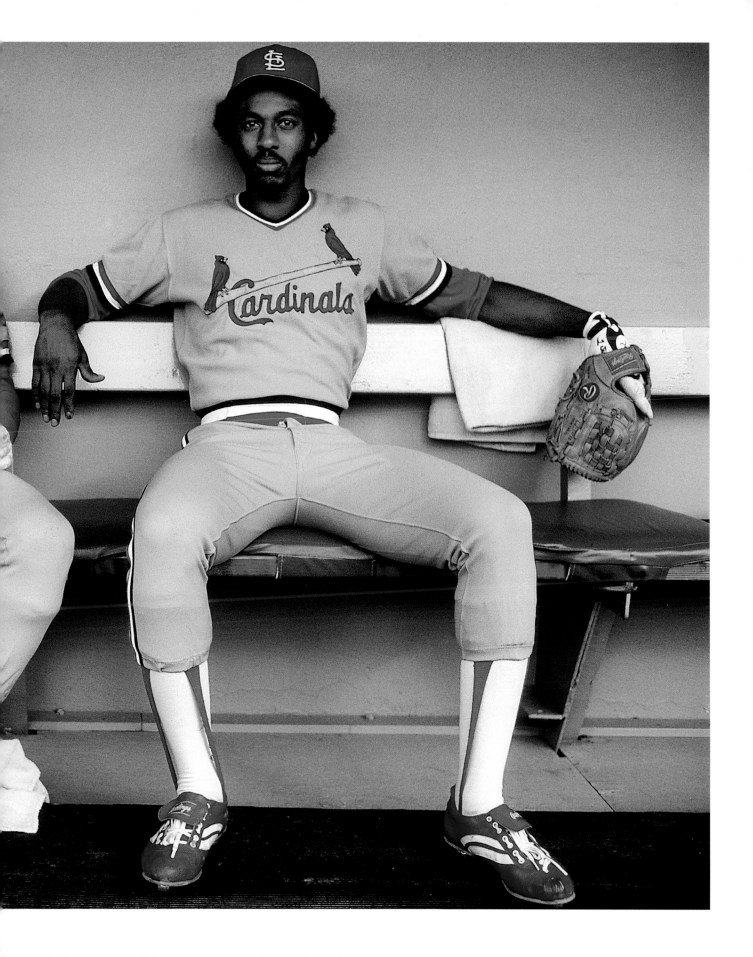

Cat. 74

W. A. Goodman & Sons (American)
Houston Astros Jersey, worn by
Joe Niekro, 1983
Polyester
83.8 × 55.9 cm (33 × 22 in.)
National Baseball Hall of Fame and
Museum, B-50-83

The pinnacle of the double knit era is
the Houston Astros' "rainbow" pullover.
Eager to rebrand the struggling team,
the Astros hired the New York ad
agency McCann Erickson to design a
new uniform. Not only was this the
firm's first time designing a uniform,
but during a period when all teams
were experimenting with new fabrics
and shapes, they were tasked with
developing "a new kind of uniform."[9]
Designer Jack Amuny began working
with strips of colored paper in various
widths, and contrary to popular belief,
he states that the stripes held no
symbolism other than a reflection of his
interest in a color sequence.[10]

Cat. 75

*Houston Astros Official Souvenir
Program and Scorebook* Cover, 1977
27.9 × 21.6 cm (11 × 8½ in.)

The cover of the 1977 Houston
Astros' program depicts the team's
colorful uniforms.

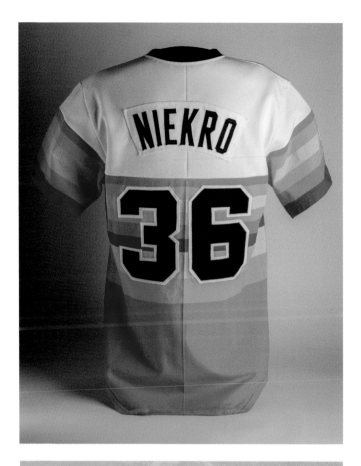

Fig. 45. An advertisement for "Turn Ahead the Clock" night at the Seattle Kingdome.

Fig. 46. Ken Griffey Jr. wearing his futuristic "Turn Ahead the Clock" jersey and silver spray-painted helmet.

Cat. 76

Majestic Athletic
(American, founded 1976)
Seattle Mariners Inaugural
"Turn Ahead the Clock" Shirt,
worn by Sam Mejias, July 18, 1998
Polyester
84.5 × 63.5 cm (33¼ × 25 in.)
National Baseball Hall of Fame and
Museum, B-155-2017

On July 18, 1998, the Seattle Mariners went to the future. Rather than joining the "Turn Back the Clock" events, for which teams played ball in retro or throwback uniforms, Kevin Martinez, the Mariners' marketing director at the time, proposed to turn the clock ahead to 2027. He pitched the idea to outfielder Ken Griffey Jr. and the veteran player responded enthusiastically to the concept, even assisting in the design of the jersey. It was "Junior" who devised the black and red color scheme and the sleeveless shirts. While the lighthearted promotion was a success, it spawned a series of league-wide "Turn Ahead the Clock" jerseys that were widely panned as a gaudy gimmick.

OFF THE FIELD

At Milan's Autumn 2018 Fashion Week, Gucci debuted a collection no one anticipated—a collaboration with Major League Baseball (MLB). San Francisco Giants and New York Yankees logos appeared on the runway as American flair for the Italian fashion house's line of outerwear and accessories. Drawing on baseball's international reach and instantly recognizable insignias, Gucci x MLB merged outlandish luxury with traditional sportswear in an unprecedented partnership. While this collection brought heightened attention to the intersection of baseball and high fashion, it is far from novel to see a baseball jersey and its accoutrements beyond the diamond and the dugout. When baseball fans began donning their favorite replica jerseys at games and sports bars, they normalized sportswear in the everyday. Without fan fashion, the baseball jersey would not carry the same pop culture status that is so appealing to designers, such as Gucci, as inspiration for off-the-field clothing ranging from streetwear to haute couture.

For fans, nostalgia arguably leads the charge in the decision to wear a baseball jersey. One's childhood experiences at a ballgame can leave a lifelong desire to recapture those initial ecstatic feelings. A Houston-based journalist reminisced over his childhood memories of watching the Astros: "Seeing greats like Nolan Ryan and guys like Mike Scott, Alan Ashby, Jim Deshaies and Billy Hatcher don those uniforms was nothing short of amazing...there were many occasions where I got to go to games and I'd just be in awe of the luminosity of the unis as well as the effervescence of our home field, fresh off [a] multi-million dollar renovation where [the] whole interior appeared to be a giant rainbow."[1] This longing to recapture the days of yore, to be a part of the fantasy on the field, and to demonstrate camaraderie and knowledge inspires many fans to wear their jerseys on game day.

Surprisingly, the baseball jersey's presence outside of the ballpark is a relatively recent phenomenon. Fans did not wear replica jerseys until the late 1970s.[2] While replica uniforms were occasionally available for children, adult fans had to get creative if they wanted to wear their team allegiance on their sleeves (literally). A plain Hanes T-shirt could become an homage to current favorite players or Hall of Fame legends with the use of markers, acrylic paint, or, for the more adventurous, a silk screen kit.[3] Local sporting goods stores saw an opportunity and began to craft their own versions of replica jerseys.[4] In 1979 athletic supplier Medalist Sand-Knit became the first manufacturer of

Fig. 47. A model wearing MIZIZI's Black Lives Matter Jersey.

licensed replica MLB jerseys. Soon fans could own and proclaim their team pride anywhere.

As the jersey grew in popularity among fans, celebrities and hip-hop stars soon gave it new cultural capital by wearing throwback and vintage replica jerseys to performances or on promotional material for their work. In particular, African American artists largely drove the shift of the jersey from fandom to casual attire. Made famous in the 1990s by Ice Cube, the Notorious B.I.G., OutKast, and Fabolous, the baseball jersey signified a new cultural uniform—one that was hip, smart, and obtainable. Jerseys were carefully chosen, sometimes as an indication of pride in a specific player or hometown, as a colorful fashion statement, or as a declaration of authenticity during a shift in the public stance toward hip-hop and its assimilation into mainstream culture.[5] To wear a replica jersey no longer solely signified sports fandom, but expanded the realm of identifiers to include the urban experience and hip-hop culture. While the throwback jersey may no longer dominate the music scene as it did in the 1990s, it maintains a stronghold in the celebrity circuit. Personalization of nameplates, numbers, and even colors has allowed some musicians, such as Bruno Mars, to completely customize their jersey and create their own "teams" while drawing on the jersey's already established street reputation and cultural significance.

Black culture has made a profound mark on the fashion world and through hip-hop brought about a crossover to streetwear. A broad style category, streetwear samples and remixes from such diverse styles as hip-hop, punk, and skateboard culture. Often rooted in self-expression, streetwear presents an opportunity to reclaim lost histories and promote socially conscious messaging. For instance, in 2017, Runaway x G Yamazawa collaborated on a jersey in honor of Japanese American ballplayers at the Heart Mountain Relocation Center, a World War II incarceration camp. And MIZIZI, a streetwear brand representing the African diaspora, designed a Black Lives Matter (BLM) jersey that has been worn by protesters across the globe. The baseball jersey, when removed from its sport context, becomes an ideological identifier on the street and a means to promote change through social commentary.

Drawn to the jersey's recognizable shape and versatility, designers have recently begun to creatively recontextualize sportswear for the runway. Freed from the realm of athletic performance and team uniformity, the baseball jersey can be repurposed to represent the identity of an individual brand as in Dolce & Gabbana's Unexpected Show from 2018, indulge in playful nostalgia with Jeremy Scott for Moschino, and serve as a beacon of diversity and inclusivity in Ashish Gupta's 2017 collection. The latter was a collaboration with Major League Baseball and is representative of the shift in the fashion industry toward the "collab." Now an essential practice for fashion houses, collaborations have brought athletic brands, celebrities, and street style together to the catwalk, generating such collections as adidas x Alexander Wang, H&M x Moschino, and Gucci x MLB. The baseball jersey of today moves seamlessly between the diamond, the runway, and everything in between, demonstrating the transformative power of this singular garment.

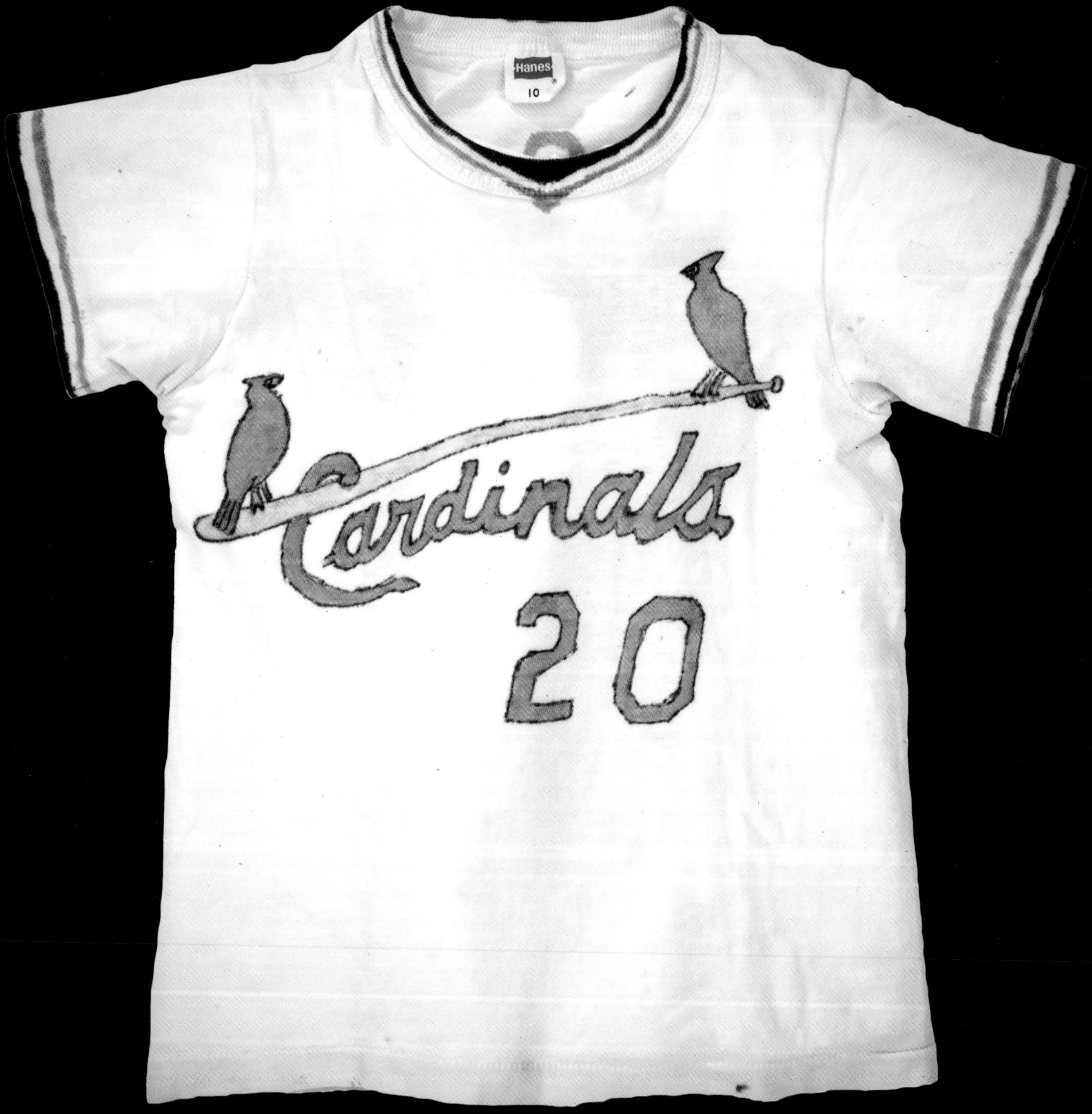
Hanes
10
Cardinals
20

Cat. 77

Larry Wentz (American, 1937–2007)
Lou Brock Jersey, St. Louis
Cardinals, ca. 1975–76
Cotton T-shirt and Magic Marker
45.7 × 33 cm (18 × 13 in.)
Courtesy of the Wentz Family

Dedicated baseball fan Larry Wentz
surprised his large family with
handmade jerseys as Christmas presents
in the mid-1970s. Using a white
Hanes T-shirt as his canvas, Wentz
painstakingly replicated contemporary
and historic jerseys with Magic Markers
and, later, acrylic paint. In order to
perfect the lettering and logos, he
often worked from baseball cards as a
reference. Player selection was crucial
as their jerseys suggested worthy
attributes for his children. These
handmade family heirlooms document
the circulation of baseball jerseys
among fans before purchasing replicas
became commonplace.

Fig. 48. Larry Wentz in his handmade Babe
Ruth jersey with his wife Lou Ann Wentz at
a party in 1998.

Cat. 78

Larry Wentz (American, 1937–2007)
César Cedeño Jersey, Houston
Astros, ca. 1975–76
Cotton T-shirt and Magic Marker
45.7 × 33 cm (18 × 13 in.)
Courtesy of the Wentz Family

Cat. 79

Larry Wentz (American, 1937–2007)
Ty Cobb Jersey, Detroit
Tigers, ca. 1975–76
Cotton T-shirt and Magic Marker
45.7 × 33 cm (18 × 13 in.)
Courtesy of the Wentz Family

Cat. 80

Larry Wentz (American, 1937–2007)
George Brett Jersey, Kansas City
Royals, ca. 1983
Cotton T-shirt and acrylic paint
45.7 × 33 cm (18 × 13 in.)
Courtesy of the Wentz Family

Cat. 81

Tabitha Soren (American, b. 1967)
Vote Pete, Cooperstown, NY, 2013
Archival pigment print
76.2 × 57.3 cm (30 × 22 9/16 in.)
Courtesy of the artist

Cat. 82

Tabitha Soren (American, b. 1967)
The Tunnel, Minneapolis, MN, 2013
Archival pigment print
76.2 × 57.3 cm (30 × 22 9/16 in.)
Courtesy of the artist

While photographing young men striving to fulfill their dream of playing in the Major Leagues, Tabitha Soren captured another side of baseball—fandom and merchandise. *Vote Pete* depicts a gift shop in Cooperstown, New York, with T-shirts and jerseys in support of Pete Rose, former Cincinnati Reds player. Rose lost his eligibility for admittance into the Hall of Fame for betting on baseball—a cardinal sin in Major League ball. Fans, however, argue that Rose deserves to be immortalized in the shrine of greats, even going so far as to wear Rose's jerseys to protest the ban. Soren also photographed tagged and plastic-wrapped Minnesota Twins jerseys hanging in the tunnel of Target Field. Here she reveals the moment before players don their new jerseys to become part of the team.

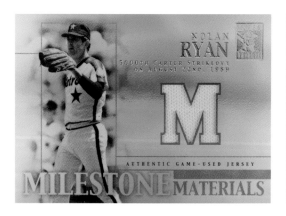

Cat. 83

The Topps Company
(American, founded 1938)
Nolan Ryan Jersey Relic
Baseball Card, 2002
Jersey swatch and cardstock
6.4 × 8.9 cm (2½ × 3½ in.)

Cat. 84

The Topps Company
(American, founded 1938)
Jason Kubel Jersey Relic
Baseball Card, 2013
Jersey swatch and cardstock
6.4 × 8.9 cm (2 ½ × 3 ½ in.)

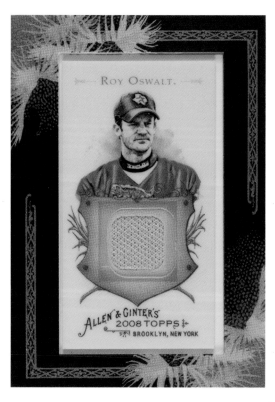

Cat. 85

The Topps Company
(American, founded 1938)
Roy Oswalt Jersey Relic
Baseball Card, 2008
Jersey swatch and cardstock
8.9 × 6.4 cm (3 ½ × 2 ½ in.)

Cat. 86

The Topps Company
(American, founded 1938)
Bret Boone Jersey Relic
Baseball Card, 2004
Jersey swatch and cardstock
8.9 × 6.4 cm (3 ½ × 2 ½ in.)

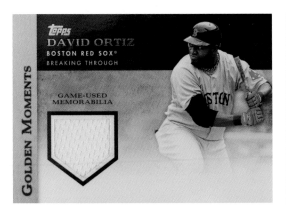

Cat. 87

The Topps Company
(American, founded 1938)
David Ortiz Jersey Relic
Baseball Card, 2012
Jersey swatch and cardstock
6.4 × 8.9 cm (2 ½ × 3 ½ in.)

Cat. 88

The Topps Company
(American, founded 1938)
Barry Bonds Jersey Relic
Baseball Card, 2002
Jersey swatch and cardstock
6.4 × 8.9 cm (2 ½ × 3 ½ in.)

Cat. 89

The Topps Company
(American, founded 1938)
Adam Dunn Jersey Relic
Baseball Card, 2008
Jersey swatch and cardstock
8.9 × 6.4 cm (3 ½ × 2 ½ in.)

Traditionally, baseball cards picture the ballplayer on the front with their statistics and bio on the back. But the advent of Upper Deck's 1997 Game Jersey inserts changed the face of baseball cards by featuring jersey swatches from Ken Griffey Jr., Tony Gwynn, and Rey Ordóñez.[1] Fans were now able to own a tangible part of baseball history—a small fragment of their players' jerseys. Touted as "game-worn," the cards are intended to bring fans even closer to the action. The popularity of baseball jersey relic cards reflects a societal shift in fandom and the marketability of memorabilia.

During the "two days that rocked the world," celebrity photographer Terry O'Neill immortalized Elton John's two sold-out concerts at Dodger Stadium in 1975. After John finished his first set, he reemerged onstage in a custom-made Bob Mackie Dodger costume as a tribute to performing at the ballpark. Mackie's design merged the traditional baseball uniform with the fantastical exuberance of the singer by creating a sequined lamé outfit proudly displaying "Elton 1" on the back. Mackie's bold interpretation set the foundation for future designers to experiment with baseball attire and is nothing short of iconic.

Cat. 90

Terry O'Neill (British, 1938–2019)
Elton John, Dodger Stadium, 1975
Archival pigment print
Courtesy of Terry O'Neill/Iconic Images

Cat. 91

Terry O'Neill (British, 1938–2019)
*Elton John, Los Angeles,
Dodger Stadium*, 1975
Archival pigment print
Courtesy of Terry O'Neill/Iconic Images

Cat. 92

Terry O'Neill (British, 1938–2019)
*Elton John, Dodger Stadium,
Batting*, 1975
Archival pigment print
Courtesy of Terry O'Neill/Iconic Images

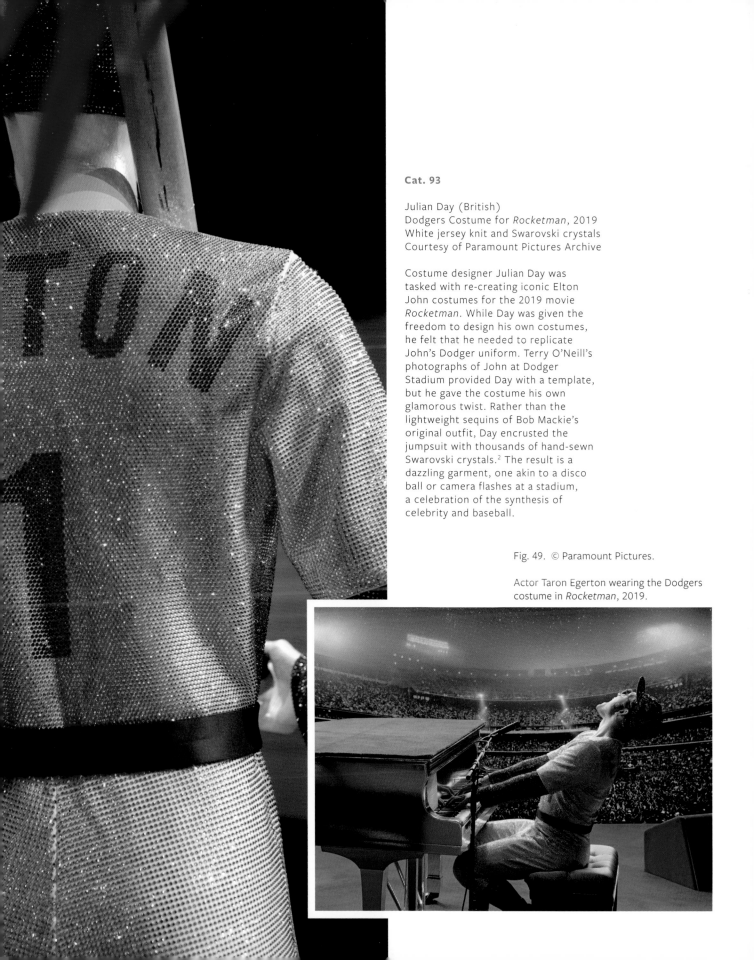

Cat. 93

Julian Day (British)
Dodgers Costume for *Rocketman*, 2019
White jersey knit and Swarovski crystals
Courtesy of Paramount Pictures Archive

Costume designer Julian Day was
tasked with re-creating iconic Elton
John costumes for the 2019 movie
Rocketman. While Day was given the
freedom to design his own costumes,
he felt that he needed to replicate
John's Dodger uniform. Terry O'Neill's
photographs of John at Dodger
Stadium provided Day with a template,
but he gave the costume his own
glamorous twist. Rather than the
lightweight sequins of Bob Mackie's
original outfit, Day encrusted the
jumpsuit with thousands of hand-sewn
Swarovski crystals.[2] The result is a
dazzling garment, one akin to a disco
ball or camera flashes at a stadium,
a celebration of the synthesis of
celebrity and baseball.

Fig. 49. © Paramount Pictures.

Actor Taron Egerton wearing the Dodgers
costume in *Rocketman*, 2019.

Cat. 94

Mitchell & Ness
(American, founded 1904)
Dale Murphy 1982 Atlanta Braves Jersey
Polyester
Courtesy of Mitchell & Ness

Mitchell & Ness began manufacturing authentic throwback jerseys of the mid-twentieth century in 1985. In 2001 one of Mitchell & Ness' customers, Reuben Harley, approached the owner, Peter Capolino, with a proposition to market to the hip-hop community. Harley saw potential after seeing Big Boi of OutKast wearing a Nolan Ryan Houston Astros jersey in the 1998 music video for Goodie Mob's "Black Ice." He convinced Capolino to produce more contemporary jerseys from the double knit era and advertised the new wares to record companies. Through Harley's grassroots efforts, Mitchell & Ness became a sensation with hip-hop stars wearing the jerseys to award ceremonies and photo shoots. Big Boi frequently wore Mitchell & Ness Atlanta Braves jerseys to represent "the spirit of Atlanta."[3]

Cat. 95

Mitchell & Ness
(American, founded 1904)
Nolan Ryan 1980 Houston Astros Jersey
Polyester
Courtesy of Mitchell & Ness

Cat. 96

Jonathan Mannion (American, b. 1970)
OutKast, Atlanta, GA,
September 8, 1998
Inkjet print on paper
Courtesy of the artist

Cat. 97

Jonathan Mannion (American, b. 1970)
Westside Connection, Los Angeles, CA,
October 8, 2003
Inkjet print on paper
Courtesy of the artist

Cat. 98

Jonathan Mannion (American, b. 1970)
Jay-Z, New York, NY, November 7, 1998
Inkjet print on paper
Courtesy of the artist

Acclaimed photographer Jonathan Mannion has captured artists in the music industry for over two decades. The baseball jersey's place in hip-hop culture is recorded in his career-defining portraits and photography for album covers. Synonymous with 1990s hip-hop, the baseball jersey's symbolism is as diverse as the music genre itself. For instance, Big Boi of OutKast often wore Atlanta Braves jerseys as a nod to his hometown. Similarly, native New Yorker Jay-Z wore Yankees apparel to show his roots and fandom pride. But a jersey could simply be a fashion statement, one with an attractive design or color scheme. Hip-hop group Westside Connection brought together noted rappers Mack 10, WC, and Ice Cube in 1996 and disbanded in 2007. Ice Cube is from Los Angeles, but has worn baseball and other sports jerseys from various teams throughout the years, and he opted to wear a retro Pittsburgh Pirates double knit jersey in the group's 2003 photograph. In 2003 when Jay-Z rapped that he swapped his jerseys for button-ups, he effectively concluded hip-hop's style obsession with the throwback jersey.[4] While today rappers occasionally wear baseball jerseys, the pinnacle of the trend remains rooted in the 1990s.

Cat. 99

Amy Page DeBlasio (American, b. 1987)
Baseball Jersey Dress,
Spring/Summer 2018
White striped polyester fabric,
multicolored polyester jacquard,
black polyester satin, and Geisha
fabric-covered shank buttons
Courtesy of the artist

Fig. 50. Baseball Jersey Dress in
Spring/Summer 2018 Lookbook.

Fig. 51. The Baseball Jersey Dress
on the runway.

Cat. 100

Amy Page DeBlasio (American, b. 1987)
Mary Print and Plaid Baseball Jersey
Dress, Autumn/Winter 2018
Cotton fabric, cotton red plaid,
black polyester satin, and blue
plastic skull buttons
Courtesy of the artist

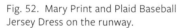

Rhode Island designer Amy Page
DeBlasio creates unexpected garments
with lush fabrics, varied textures, and
bold prints. Her luxury streetwear
challenges the monotony of everyday
casual clothing. DeBlasio's Mary Dress
consists of two distinct fabrics: plaid
and a print of Our Lady of Guadalupe,
a contrast that almost obscures the
baseball jersey shape of the garment.
Her Baseball Jersey Dress (Cat. 99)
more directly references the baseball
jersey with her brand name and
collection year on the back. Designed
for two different collections, these
garments demonstrate how broadly
the baseball jersey has inspired fashion
design, from the readily apparent to
the more abstract.

Fig. 52. Mary Print and Plaid Baseball
Jersey Dress on the runway.

Cat. 101

Louis Vuitton by Kim Jones × Supreme
(Look 10), Fall/Winter 2017
Denim monogram short-sleeve overshirt
Denim
Paris, Collection Louis Vuitton

A collaboration of global proportions,
Louis Vuitton × Supreme brought
together an unlikely pairing of the Paris
maison and the New York skate brand.
Unveiled at Paris Fashion Week in 2017,
the men's Autumn/Winter collection
debuted co-branded clothing adorned
with LV's signature monogram and
Supreme's box logo. One of the key
pieces in the collection was the denim
jacquard baseball jersey. Employing
the iconic jersey shape, the garment
displays the intricately woven patterns
of the dual brands in sturdy twill-
weave cotton, a fabric utterly unsuited
to baseball but indicative of current
streetwear trends.

Fig. 53. Model at Milan Men's Fashion
Week, Spring/Summer 2020.

Cat. 102

Moschino × H&M
Baseball Dress, 2018
Polyester

Moschino's creative director, Jeremy
Scott, devised a collaboration between
the Italian fashion house and the fast
fashion Swedish retail brand H&M.
Drawing on Scott's 2015 Moschino
collection, this collaboration features
the designer's trademark "cartoon
couture" and branded logos. Inspired
by the nostalgia of cartoons, especially
Disney, Scott flaunts vintage Americana
in a celebration of consumerism and
the democratization of fashion. The
baseball jersey dress displays classic
Disney characters, the Moschino logo,
and a label tag declaring the garment
was "engineered exclusively for high
fashion & fun." Reminiscent of the
all-American pastime, the collection's
jersey dress celebrates play over
rivalrous competition.

Fig. 54. Moschino × H&M on the runway.

Cat. 103

BAPE × Mitchell & Ness
New York Mets Baseball Jersey, 2019
Polyester
Courtesy of Mitchell & Ness

Known for creating vintage throwback jerseys, Mitchell & Ness also create originals with their brand collaborations. Japanese streetwear brand A Bathing Ape, also known as BAPE, worked with Mitchell & Ness to develop a capsule MLB-inspired collection from four teams: the New York Yankees, Los Angeles Angels, New York Mets, and Los Angeles Dodgers. The teams were selected based on BAPE US store locations and as a "nod to the camaraderie and rivalry between the two cities."[5] The button-down Mets jersey features the iconic BAPE camo print, a distorted BAPE ape floating among amorphous shapes, and the brand's founding year ('93) on the back. This collaboration also gestures to the long history and popularity of baseball in Japan.

Cat. 104

Ebbets Field Flannels
(American, founded 1988)
Kansas City Monarchs 1942 Home
Baseball Jersey
Wool flannel

After feeling dissatisfied with his inability to find vintage jerseys, Jerry Cohen founded Ebbets Field Flannels in 1988 to make his own jerseys. Unable to manufacture MLB jerseys without an official license, Cohen shifted his sights to the minor leagues and Negro Leagues. Much like the flannel days of yore, each jersey is custom-made to order and meticulously researched for accuracy, producing work once likened to American folk art.[6] The prominent and successful Kansas City Monarchs went through several uniforms during their thirty-seven seasons, but are often associated with their vibrant red and white uniforms from 1942. In that year the team won the Negro League World Series with pitcher Satchel Paige, whose number "25" is represented on the back of the uniform.

Fig. 55. Kansas City Monarchs, 1942, National Baseball Hall of Fame and Museum, BL-1522-72.

Kansas City Monarchs with Satchel Paige on the far right in 1942.

Cat. 105

Runaway × G Yamazawa
Heart Mountain Baseball Jersey, 2017
Double knit heavyweight polyester
Courtesy of Runaway × G Yamazawa

Streetwear company Runaway and rapper G Yamazawa collaborated on a baseball jersey to promote awareness of Japanese American ballplayers during World War II. Forcibly removed to incarceration camps during the war, Japanese Americans played baseball behind barbed wire as a diversion and to display their patriotism. One internee, Takeo Suo, recalled: "Putting on a baseball uniform was like wearing the American flag."[7] As players wore their jerseys from their home teams, Runaway and G Yamazawa designed a retro-inspired jersey to honor the baseball team at the Heart Mountain Relocation Center in Wyoming. The short-sleeved button-down has black-and-white pinstripes and the back of the jersey reads "'42"—an abbreviation of the year Heart Mountain opened.

Fig. 56. Mori Shimida, Heart Mountain, Wyoming, 1942–45, Japanese American National Museum, Mori Shimida Collection, 92.10.2DF.

Baseball players at Heart Mountain in different uniforms in a photograph dated between 1942 and 1945.

Fig. 57. G Yamazawa wearing the Heart Mountain Jersey.

Cat. 106

MIZIZI (American, founded 2015)
Ghana Baseball Jersey
Polyester
Courtesy of MIZIZI International, LLC

Founded in 2015 by Ghanaian American Paakow Essandoh, MIZIZI, which means "roots" in Swahili, designs sports jerseys to connect people to their cultural ties and to one another across the globe. Dubbed the official streetwear brand of the African diaspora, MIZIZI offers jerseys representing countries throughout Africa, Latin America, and the Caribbean. Each jersey design undergoes careful vetting, according to Essandoh: "Whenever we're in the designing process, we talk to people from said communities and add in any cultural nuances to the design to ensure that when someone wears it, they feel genuinely represented."[8] For instance, the Ghana Jersey displays kente cloth patterns; the Gye Nyame symbol (meaning the supremacy of God); and, on the back, 1957, the year of Ghana's independence.

Fig. 58. Models wearing MIZIZI baseball jerseys.

Fig. 59. A model showing the back of the Ghana Jersey.

Cat. 107

MIZIZI (American, founded 2015)
Black Lives Matter Jersey
Polyester
Courtesy of MIZIZI International, LLC

In addition to representing distinct countries of the African diaspora, MIZIZI also designs jerseys for the Black Lives Matter movement. Released in 2016 as demonstrations swept the United States in response to the murders of Alton Sterling and Philando Castile, among many others at the hands of police officers, the BLM jersey was designed to support another aspect of the diaspora. To acknowledge Ghana's place at the center of the transatlantic slave trading route, one sleeve depicts the Adinkra symbol of *Sankofa* for growth and reflection. The other sleeve shows the Black power fist for solidarity. "1865" on the back of the jersey represents the year of emancipation from chattel slavery.

Fig. 60. A model wearing the Black Lives Matter Jersey.

Cat. 108

Gucci (Italian, founded 1921)
Duchesse Shirt, Spring/Summer 2017
Acetate and embroidered appliqué

For Gucci's Spring/Summer 2017
collection, "Magic Lanterns,"
creative director Alessandro Michele
devised a romantic fairy tale full of
extravagance and a sporty aesthetic.
Michele wrote in the show notes: "The
clothes tell a story steeped in wonder,
phantasmagoria and unorthodoxy. Such
stories don't mimetically represent
reality. They rather act as magic
lanterns, as distorting mirrors, altering
languages, signs and consolidated
codes."[9] In this way, the Duchesse
Shirt reflects the American-style
baseball shirt without obvious visual
references to Major League Baseball.
In a nod to Gucci's traditional designs,
the shirt features the fashion house's
signature stripes around the button
placket and armholes.

Fig. 61. On the runway at Milan
Fashion Week.

Cat. 110

Ashish (British, founded 2001)
New York Mets Shirt and Pants,
Autumn/Winter 2017
Sequins and beads on cotton; sequins
and beads on silk georgette
Courtesy of Ashish

Delhi-born, London-based designer
Ashish Gupta drew inspiration from
America's favorite pastime for his
Autumn/Winter 2017 collection.
Collaborating with Major League
Baseball, Gupta envisioned a fanciful
universe filled with glitter and glam
to make a statement about inclusivity
amid a tense global political climate.
Gupta's trademark sequins shared the
catwalk with MLB logos and optimistic
slogans such as "unity in adversity." The
unisex garments merge the traditional
sporty uniform with Gupta's distinct
vision of positivity, all in an American
patriotic palette. As Gupta researched
the American sport, he said, "I didn't
know the rich heritage of the game—
the teams, the way it brought a range
of communities together in its early
days. It was a game of the people,
of immigrants."[10]

Cat. 111

Darren Romanelli (DRx/Dr. Romanelli)
(American, b. 1967)
One-of-a-Kind Baseball Jersey Chair,
Los Angeles Dodgers, 2020
Reconstructed jerseys with Major
League Baseball
Courtesy of the artist and Major
League Baseball

Los Angeles designer Darren Romanelli, known as DRx or Dr. Romanelli, reconceives the baseball jersey beyond a garment to be worn. In his clothing-to-furniture transformations, Romanelli takes upcycled MLB jerseys and crafts one-of-a-kind chairs, featuring the jersey's iconic button placket, team names, and logos of the MLB and Majestic Athletic. Romanelli deconstructs Los Angeles Dodgers

and Boston Red Sox jerseys and uses the teams' logos as the anchor pieces around which other parts of the jersey are used to rebuild the garment anew. These bespoke chairs enable fans to experience the baseball jersey in an entirely new fashion as a means to consider sustainability with a streetwear vibe.

Cat. 112

Darren Romanelli (DRx/Dr. Romanelli)
(American, b. 1967)
One-of-a-Kind Baseball Jersey Chair,
Boston Red Sox, 2020
Reconstructed jerseys with Major
League Baseball
Courtesy of the artist and Major
League Baseball

NOTES

Behind the Seams

1. Opening monologue of *Seinfeld*, season 6, episode 11, "The Label Maker," aired January 19, 1995.
2. "Fan's 'Fraud' Shirt Creates a Stir," ESPN.com, July 26, 2013, https://www.espn.com/mlb/story/_/id/9511475/milwaukee-brewers-fan-forced-cover-ryan-braun-fraud-jersey.
3. Recent instances include Bryce Harper and Robinson Canó: see Mikaela Lefrak, "Nationals Fans React to Bryce Harper's Return to D.C. with Anger and Artistry," *WAMU*, April 2, 2019, https://wamu.org/story/19/04/02/nationals-fans-react-to-bryce-harpers-return-to-d-c-with-anger-and-artistry/; and Tristan Thornburgh, "Yankees Fan Burns Robinson Cano Jersey," *Bleacher Report*, December 6, 2013, https://bleacherreport.com/articles/1879185-yankees-fan-burns-robinson-cano-jersey.
4. Henry Chadwick, "The Uniform of Clubs," *Beadle's Dime Base-Ball Player* (New York: Beadle, 1869), 99.
5. "D. & M. Uniforms," *The Lucky Dog Kind* (New Hampshire: Draper and Maynard, Spring and Summer 1924): 34.
6. Stephen Patrick Andon, "Sporting Materiality: Commodification and Fan Agency in Collections, Memorabilia, Jerseys, and Dirt" (PhD diss., Florida State University, 2011), 71.
7. Charles A. Peverelly, *The Book of American Pastimes: Containing a History of the Principal Base Ball, Cricket, Rowing, and Yachting Clubs of the United States* (New York, 1866), 344.
8. See, for instance, a 1921 advertisement for baseball attire that distinguishes "baseball sweaters" from "baseball jerseys." Advertisement for Reinhart's Department Store, *Tribune* (Scranton, PA), May 19, 1921, 18.
9. Several essays cover this debate, but I found the following particularly informative: Paola Antonelli, "Who's Afraid of Fashion?," in *ITEMS: Is Fashion Modern?*, ed. Paola Antonelli and Michelle Millar Fisher (New York: Museum of Modern Art, 2017), 15–22.
10. Tom Lepperd, ed., *Official Baseball Rules*, 2019 edition (Major League Baseball, 2019), 6–7.
11. There have been several studies on the psychology of sports fans and the physical effects of fandom. See, for instance, Brian J. Barth, "The Unique Neurology of the Sports Fan's Brain," *Nautilus*, August 11, 2016, http://nautil.us/issue/39/sport/the-unique-neurology-of-the-sports-fans-brain.
12. For the concept of bricolage, see Claude Lévi-Strauss, *The Savage Mind*, trans. George Weidenfeld (Chicago: University of Chicago Press, 1966), 16–30. For the application of bricolage to street culture, see Dick Hebdige, *Subculture: The Meaning of Style* (London: Methuen, 1979), 103–5.
13. Donnie Kwak, "Throwbacks Instant Vintage," *Vibe*, September 2003, 218.
14. As of December 16, 2020, Commissioner of Baseball Robert D. Manfred, Jr. announced that Major League Baseball designates the Negro Leagues as having 'Major League' status. Major League Baseball, MLB officially designates the Negro Leagues as 'Major League', 2020, https://www.mlb.com/press-release/press-release-mlb-officially-designates-the-negro-leagues-as-major-league.
15. Paul Lukas, "Gross: MLB Reveals Full Slate of Nike-fied Home Jerseys," *Uni Watch*, December 10, 2019, https://uni-watch.com/2019/12/10/gross-mlb-reveals-full-slate-of-nike-fied-home-jerseys/.
16. It should be noted that the first instance of the iconic NY monogram occurred four years before the Tiffany & Co.–inspired design graced the front of the uniform. Todd Radom, "Interlocked, Intertwined, Interesting," *Todd Radom Design*, September 19, 2017, https://www.toddradom.com/blog/5380; and Richard Morgan, "A Salute Not to the Yankees, But to Their Logo," *New York Times*, September 30, 2013, https://cityroom.blogs.nytimes.com/2013/09/30/a-salute-not-to-the-yankees-but-to-their-logo/.
17. Tom Shieber of the National Baseball Hall of Fame doubts Devery's role and the inspiration. Tom Shieber, "That Famous Yankees Logo," *Baseball Researcher*, April 12, 2010, http://baseballresearcher.blogspot.com/2010/03/that-famous-yankees-logo.html.
18. Todd Radom, "The Cleveland Indians—and Chief Wahoo—Return to the October Stage," *Todd Radom Design*, October 17, 2016, https://www.toddradom.com/blog/2016-cleveland-indians-chief-wahoo-veeck.
19. David Waldstein, "Cleveland Indians Will Abandon Chief Wahoo Next Year," *New York Times*, January 29, 2018, https://www.nytimes.com/2018/01/29/sports/baseball/cleveland-indians-chief-wahoo-logo.html.
20. That said, several notable players have worn numbers fifty and above: Randy Johnson, Ichiro Suzuki, and Bernie Williams all wore #51.
21. Recently traded Roger Clemens paid Blue Jays teammate Carlos Delgado to switch numbers in 1997. This is just one of several examples of players keeping their numbers after joining a new team or because of a symbolic significance to the numbers.
22. "Number Players for Benefit of Fans," *Indianapolis News*, June 27, 1916, 14.
23. The Yankees announced the decision and the Cleveland Indians followed suit a few weeks later. Because the Yankees' opening day was rained out, the Indians were the first Major League team to wear numbers on their backs.
24. "New York Yankees Wear Numbers on Back," *Altoona Mirror*, January 23, 1929, 20.
25. Originally designed for the 1951 World Series, the Dodgers lost the playoffs to the New York Giants and never got to wear the new uniforms. Todd Radom, "The Tale of the Dodgers' Red Uniform Numbers and the 'Shot Heard 'Round the World,'" *Todd Radom Design*, October 15, 2013, https://www.toddradom.com/blog/the-tale-of-the-dodgers-red-uniform-numbers-and-the-shot-heard-round-the-world. Also

cited in "Once over Lightly," *Herald and Review* (Decatur, IL), April 30, 1952, 13; and "Charley Frey Leads Triplets [*sic*] Hitters with Gaudy .423," *Press and Sun-Bulletin* (Binghamton, NY), May 3, 1952, 11.

26. The first color televised baseball game was the Brooklyn Dodgers against the Boston Braves on August 11, 1951.

27. Retiring numbers is not limited to players; it can also include coaches, managers, and umpires.

28. Kerr Houston, "Athletic Iconography in Spike Lee's Early Films," *African American Review* 38, no. 4 (Winter 2004): 640–42.

29. Advertisement for Spalding baseball uniforms in T. H. Murnane, ed., *Official Guide of the National Association of Professional Base Ball Leagues* (New York: American Sports Publishing, 1912).

30. Liz Daus and Marcia Meyer (R. J. Liebe Athletic Lettering Company), interview with the author, September 8, 2020.

31. David Butwin, "Baseball Flannels Are Hot: Faithful Reproductions of Classic Jerseys Are Setting a Trend in Philadelphia," *Sports Illustrated*, July 6, 1987, 105, https://vault.si.com/vault/1987/07/06/baseball-flannels-are-hot-faithful-reproductions-of-classic-jerseys-are-setting-a-trend-in-philadelphia.

32. Jay Feldman, "Flannel Jerseys to Order: Jerry Cohen Does Brisk Trade in Authentic Replicas," *Sports Illustrated*, July 30, 1990, 8, https://vault.si.com/vault/1990/07/30/flannel-jerseys-to-order.

33. Alex Lendrum, "Dr. Romanelli Is the Mad Scientist of Vintage Clothing," *Hypebeast*, February 15, 2016, https://hypebeast.com/2016/2/dr-romanelli-hypebeast-magazine-interview.

The Modern Jersey

1. "Check Out the Nike Jerseys for Major League Baseball," *Nike News*, December 9, 2019, https://news.nike.com/news/nike-x-major-league-baseball-uniforms-2020-official-images.

2. Charles A. Peverelly, *The Book of American Pastimes: Containing a History of the Principal Base Ball, Cricket, Rowing, and Yachting Clubs of the United States* (New York, 1866), 344.

3. *Princeton Alumni Weekly* 4, no. 36 (June 18, 1904): 624.

4. *New York Evening World*, March 6, 1906, 12.

5. "You May Not Tell Teams by Their Uniforms," *Lawrence Journal-World*, March 29, 1987, cited in Todd Radom, "1987—The Year That MLB's Uniforms Stepped Backwards," *Todd Radom Design*, June 13, 2013, https://www.toddradom.com/blog/1987-the-year-that-mlbs-uniforms-stepped-backwards.

6. Sarah Ballard, "The Fabric of the Game," *Sports Illustrated*, April 5, 1989.

7. Cam Wolf, "It's Time to Pull the Baseball Uniform into the 21st Century," *Racked*, April 6, 2017, https://www.racked.com/2017/4/6/15168578/rebuild-baseball-uniform.

The Modern Jersey — Plates

1. An amateur team organized in 1857, the Tri-Mountains were the first Massachusetts club to adopt the New York variant of baseball, a style popularized by the Knickerbockers that was the forerunner of modern baseball. David Mihaly, "When Baseball Was Square," *Verso* (blog), Huntington Library, Art Museum, and Botanical Gardens, June 30, 2016, https://www.huntington.org/verso/2018/08/when-baseball-was-square.

2. John A. Blanchard, ed., *The H Book of Harvard Athletics, 1852–1922* (Cambridge, MA: Harvard Varsity Club: 1923), 148.

3. A photograph of the Burr and Burton Academy football team at the Bennington Museum dating to the same time period, taken by the same photographer, suggests the uniforms were worn for multiple sports. See Burr and Burton Football Team, Bennington Museum, 1990.139.8.

4. "Discard 'Red Sox' Insignia," *Chicago Tribune*, December 23, 1908, 10.

5. Peter Devereaux, *Game Faces: Early Baseball Cards from the Library of Congress* (Washington, DC: Smithsonian Books, 2018), 86.

6. *Spalding's Official Base Ball Guide* (New York: American Sports Publishing, 1911), 870.

7. Wayne Maurice Ladd, "The Athletic Institute: A Study of an Organization and Its Effects on and Reflection of the Development of Sport, Recreation, and Physical Education in the United States" (PhD diss., Ohio State University, 1974), 18.

8. "Fisher at Tudor Park," *Bennington Banner*, June 9, 1911, 1.

9. Ernie Wright Jr., the owner's son, wore this jersey while he was a batboy for the team.

10. Liz Daus and Marcia Meyer (R. J. Liebe Athletic Lettering Company), interview with the author, September 8, 2020.

11. "Stall & Dean to Establish Branch Here," *Daily Times* (Davenport, IA), March 10, 1929, 26.

12. Tim McAuliffe entered an exclusive deal with Stall & Dean in 1952 to produce uniforms under the McAuliffe name, and following McAuliffe's death Stall & Dean continued the brand but under the name McAuliffe Uniform Company.

13. Randy Skubek, "He Is a She," *Latrobe Bulletin*, October 30, 1990, 12.

14. Tabitha Soren, *Fantasy Life: Baseball and the American Dream* (New York: Aperture, 2017).

15. Jen McCaffrey, "The Story behind the Rare 'Boston' Jerseys the Red Sox Wear on Patriots Day," *Athletic*, April 15, 2019, https://theathletic.com/923811/2019/04/15/the-story-behind-the-rare-boston-jerseys-the-red-sox-wear-on-patriots-day/.

16. Irving Perez, "Fuji Athletics" (MS thesis, University of Oregon, 2018), 11.

Experimental Design

1. For a delightful account of the "ugly" baseball jerseys over the years, see Todd Radom, *Winning Ugly: A Visual History of the Most Bizarre Baseball Uniforms Ever Worn* (New York: Sports Publishing, 2018).
2. Harry Grayson, "The Payoff," *Santa Ana Register*, May 1, 1940, 8.
3. Kristie Rieken, "Rainbow Resurgence: Bright Astros Jerseys Now a Fan Favorite," *Associated Press*, October 27, 2017.
4. Alan Siegel, "How Mitchell & Ness Built an Empire and Launched the Golden Age of Sports Nostalgia," *USA Today*, July 15, 2015, https://ftw.usatoday.com/2015/07/throwback-jersey-mitchell-ness-toronto-raptors.
5. *Spalding's Official Base Ball Guide* (Saint Louis, MO: Horton, 1882), 92–93; and "Sporting Matters," *Detroit Free Press*, December 11, 1881, 4, cited in Peter Morris, *A Game of Inches: The Stories Behind the Innovations That Shaped Baseball* (Chicago: Ivan Roe, 2010), 315.
6. Morris, *Game of Inches*, 316; and *Albany Argus*, July 7, 1882, cited in Craig Brown, "1882 Chicago," *Threads of Our Game*, https://www.threadsofourgame.com/1882-chicago/.
7. Night games were the brainchild of Cincinnati Reds manager Leland Stanford "Larry" MacPhail, starting with the first night game at Crosley Field on May 24, 1935.
8. Jack Cuddy, "Bums' Fans to See Satin Uniforms Tonight; Lip Near 'Berling Pernt,'" *Nashville Banner*, May 23, 1944, 15; Harry Grason, "Dodgers from Rags to Rickey; Satin Uniforms Are Result of Girls' Ball Influence," *Kenosha Evening News*, March 1, 1944, 8; and Jerry Nason, "Dazzling Electric Display from 8 Towers Illuminates Park for Game with Giants," *Boston Globe*, May 12, 1946, 1. Grason incorrectly cites the All-American Girls Professional Baseball League as a softball team, an error indicative of the sexism present in the sport.
9. An article on Boston Braves manager Billy Southworth and the Horace Partridge & Co. factory stated that the satin "didn't absorb perspiration as flannel does and proved impractical": "Billy Southworth So Particular about Braves' Streamlined Uniforms He Has Bagginess Taken Out of Knees of Pants," *Boston Globe*, July 3, 1949, 82.
10. Radom, *Winning Ugly*, 57–75.
11. "Braves Modernize Garb," *Panama City News-Herald*, February 13, 1972, 15. Also cited in Radom, *Winning Ugly*, 57.
12. Dick Meister, "Finley Responsible for Colorful Uniforms," *Asbury Park Press*, October 19, 1982, 47.
13. Paul Lukas, "A Look Back at the Mariners' Futuristic Night," ESPN.com, July 21, 2008, https://www.espn.com/espn/page2/story?page=lukas/080718.
14. "Baseball the Way It Could Sorta Be in 2021," *Saint Louis Post-Dispatch*, July 25, 1999, 22.
15. Lukas, "Look Back"; and "The Future of Baseball Uniforms Is Not Pretty," *South Florida Sentinel*, June 28, 1999, 22.
16. Adam Jude, "Mariners Get in the Spirit for Second Turn Ahead the Clock Night," *Seattle Times*, June 30, 2018.

Experimental Design — Plates

1. "Boston Gets on Beam as Braves Dedicate New Arcs," *Sporting News*, May 16, 1946, 7.
2. Francis Sargent, "The Lookout," *Lowell Sun*, August 27, 1947, 31.
3. Anika Orrock, *The Incredible Women of the All-American Girls Professional Baseball League* (New York: Chronicle Books, 2020), 30, 33.
4. R. J. Liebe Athletic Lettering Company formed a partnership with Rawlings in 1935 for all the lettering on their uniforms. Each Liebe worker performed specific roles in the embroidery process. One woman, Eulah Street, only embroidered the birds' beaks and stitched the players' names

on their tails. Liz Daus and Marcia Meyer (R. J. Liebe Athletic Lettering Company), interview with the author, September 8, 2020.
5. For a history of the zipper, see Robert Friedel, *Zipper: An Exploration in Novelty* (New York: W. W. Norton, 1994).
6. One newspaper claimed that it was because of Pirates player Ted Kluszewski's "gargantuan hams for arms" that the shift from traditional jerseys to sleeveless ones occurred. Vince Leonard, "Sports Vignettes," *Daily Republican* (Monongahela, PA), August 29, 1959, 6.
7. Russell Drumm, "An Affair with a Moment," *Graphis*, November 1, 1998, 78.
8. Art Holliday, "*Sports Illustrated* Photographer Reflects on His St. Louis Photos," *KSDK*, September 14, 2018, https://www.ksdk.com/article/features/sports-illustrated-photographer-reflects-on-his-st-louis-photos/63-594428322.
9. Paul Lukas, "The Exclusive Untold Story behind the Astros' Rainbow Uniform," ESPN.com, August 2, 2017, https://www.espn.com/mlb/story/_/id/20219881/the-history-houston-iconic-rainbow-uniforms-story-worth-telling.
10. Lukas, "Exclusive Untold Story."

Off the Field

1. Brian K. Patterson, "Houston Astros Report: The Evolution of the Rainbow Uniform Reveled," *House of Houston*, August 5, 2017, https://houseofhouston.com/2017/08/05/houston-astros-report-evolution-rainbow-uniform-revealed/.
2. The first adult fans wearing replica jerseys appeared in the early 1970s, but for the National Hockey League. Baseball seems to have come a bit later. By 1987 *Sports Illustrated* ran a story about Mitchell & Ness, a replica jersey company, and the rise of reproduction jerseys. See David Butwin, "Baseball Flannels Are Hot," *Sports Illustrated*,

July 6, 1987, 115.

3. Even among the variety of authentic replica jersey options today, some fans continue to DIY their jerseys. Only instead of creating out of necessity, today's DIYers are motivated by circumventing the commercialization of baseball, creative control over custom apparel, and affordability. See Stephen Patrick Andon, "Sewing It Alone: Uniform DIYers in the Hypermasculine World of Sports Fandom," in "Sporting Materiality: Commodification and Fan Agency in Collections, Memorabilia, Jerseys, and Dirt" (PhD diss., Florida State University, 2011), 111–25.

4. This happens even today, as it did with the announcement of the move of the Pawtucket Red Sox to Worcester, Massachusetts. George Barnes, "After PawSox Announcement, Guertin Graphics in Worcester Begins Making Shirt and Hats," *Worcester Telegram & Gazette*, August 20, 2018, https://www.telegram.com/news/20180820/after-pawsox-announcement-guertin-graphics-in-worcester-begins-making-shirt-and-hats.

5. Elena Romero, *Free Stylin': How Hip Hop Changed the Fashion Industry* (Santa Barbara, CA: Praeger, 2012), 137–39; and Cory Hillman, *American Sports in the Age of Consumption: How Commercialization Is Changing the Game* (Jefferson, NC: McFarland, 2016), 136–40.

June 22, 2018, https://www.facebook.com/Braves/videos/10155771849947831.

4. Jay-Z, "What More Can I Say," *The Black Album*, 2003, Def Jam Recordings and Roc-A-Fella Records.

5. BAPE, "BAPE® x Mitchell & Ness," press release, BAPE, 2018, https://us.bape.com/blogs/news/bape-x-mitchell-ness.

6. George Weigel, "Take Me Out to the Real Ballgame," *Los Angeles Times*, April 5, 1994, 5.

7. Kerry Yo Nakagawa, *Through a Diamond: 100 Years of Japanese American Baseball* (San Francisco: Rudi Publishing, 2001), 27.

8. Bonita, "We Caught Up with Founder of African Diaspora Streetwear Brand MIZIZI," *GUAP*, April 23, 2020, https://guap.co.uk/we-caught-up-with-founder-of-african-diaspora-streetwear-brand-mizizishop/.

9. Dhani Mau, "Gucci's Alessandro Michele Sucks Us into His Hazy, All-Pink World for Spring," *Fashionista*, September 21, 2016, https://fashionista.com/2016/09/gucci-spring-2017-review.

10. "We Don't Need Another Hero," *Wonderland*, August 18, 2018, https://www.wonderlandmagazine.com/2017/08/18/dont-need-another-hero/.

Off the Field — Plates

1. Upper Deck started with football jersey cards in 1996.

2. Rachel Lee Harris, "Goodbye Yellow Lycra: See Elton John's 'Rocketman' Looks Up Close," *New York Times*, June 17, 2019, https://www.nytimes.com/2019/06/17/movies/rocketman-elton-john-costumes.html.

3. Atlanta Braves, "Big Boi Reflects on the Atlanta Braves," *Facebook*, video, 1:20,

SELECTED BIBLIOGRAPHY

Adz, King, and Wilma Stone. *This Is Not Fashion: Streetwear Past and Present*. New York: Thames & Hudson, 2018.

Andon, Stephen Patrick. "Rooting for the Clothes: The Materialization of Memory in Baseball's Throwback Uniforms." *Nine: A Journal of Baseball History and Culture* 21, no. 2 (Spring 2013): 32–55.

———. "Sporting Materiality: Commodification and Fan Agency in Collections, Memorabilia, Jerseys, and Dirt." PhD diss., Florida State University, 2011.

Antonelli, Paola, and Michelle Millar Fisher. *ITEMS: Is Fashion Modern?* New York: Museum of Modern Art, 2018.

Ballard, Sarah. "The Fabric of the Game." *Sports Illustrated*, April 5, 1989, 108–18.

Bartkowiak, Mathew J., and Yuya Kiuchi. *Packaging Baseball: How Marketing Embellishes the Cultural Experience*. Jefferson, NC: McFarland, 2012.

Brown, Craig. "Threads of Our Game." *Threads of Our Game: 19th-Century Baseball Uniform Database*, 2014. https://www.threadsofourgame.com/.

Brown, Patricia Leigh. "Pine Tar Couture." *New York Times*, July 18, 1993, section 9, 1.

Butwin, David. "Baseball Flannels Are Hot: Faithful Reproductions of Classic Jerseys Are Setting a Trend in Philadelphia." *Sports Illustrated*, July 6, 1987, 105.

Chadwick, Henry, ed. *Beadle's Dime Base-Ball Player*. New York: Beadle, 1869.

Craik, Jennifer. *The Face of Fashion: Cultural Studies in Fashion*. New York: Thames & Hudson, 2003.

———. *Uniforms Exposed: From Conformity to Transgression*. New York: Berg, 2005.

DeLeon, Jian, Robert Klanten, and Marie-Elisabeth Niebius. *The Incomplete: Highsnobiety Guide to Street Fashion and Culture*. Berlin: Gestalten, 2018.

Devereaux, Peter. *Game Faces: Early Baseball Cards from the Library of Congress*. Washington, DC: Smithsonian Books, 2018.

Dreifort, John E., ed. *Baseball History from Outside the Lines: A Reader*. Lincoln: University of Nebraska Press, 2001.

Feldman, Jay. "Flannel Jerseys to Order: Jerry Cohen Does Brisk Trade in Authentic Replicas." *Sports Illustrated*, July 30, 1990, 8.

Freeman, Rodney, Katherine C. Donahue, Eric Baxter, Patrick J. Collins, Marie Connell, and Steven Kantor. "The Draper-Maynard Sporting Goods Company of Plymouth, New Hampshire, 1840–1937." *IA: The Journal for the Society for Industrial Archaeology* 21, nos. 1–2 (1994): 139–51.

Friedel, Robert. *Zipper: An Exploration in Novelty*. New York: W. W. Norton, 1994.

Goldstein, Warren. *Playing for Keeps: A History of Early Baseball*. Ithaca: Cornell University Press, 1989.

Hebdige, Dick. *Subculture: The Meaning of Style*. London: Methuen, 1979.

Hillman, Cory. *American Sports in the Age of Consumption: How Commercialization Is Changing the Game*. Jefferson, NC: McFarland, 2016.

Houston, Kerr. "Athletic Iconography in Spike Lee's Early Films." *African American Review* 38, no. 4 (Winter 2004): 637–49.

Levine, Peter. *A. G. Spalding and the Rise of Baseball: The Promise of American Sport*. New York: Oxford University Press, 1985.

Lukas, Paul. "The Exclusive Untold Story behind the Astros' Rainbow Uniform."
ESPN.com, August 2, 2017. https://www.espn.com/mlb/story/_/id/20219881/the-history-houston-iconic-rainbow-uniforms-story-worth-telling.

McCormack, Louise Samaha. *The Draper and Maynard Sporting Goods Company: A Community Yesterday, Today, and Tomorrow*. 2017.

Morris, Peter. *A Game of Inches: The Stories Behind the Innovations That Shaped Baseball*. Chicago: Ivan Roe, 2010.

Nakagawa, Kerry Yo. *Through a Diamond: 100 Years of Japanese American Baseball*. San Francisco: Rudi Publishing, 2001.

Okkonen, Marc. *Baseball Uniforms of the 20th Century*. New York: Sterling Publishing, 1991.

Orrock, Anika. *The Incredible Women of the All-American Girls Professional Baseball League*. New York: Chronicle Books, 2020.

Perez, Irving. "Fuji Athletics." MS thesis, University of Oregon, 2018.

Peverelly, Charles A. *The Book of American Pastimes: Containing a History of the Principal Base Ball, Cricket, Rowing, and Yachting Clubs of the United States*. New York, 1866.

Radom, Todd. *Winning Ugly: A Visual History of the Most Bizarre Baseball Uniforms Ever Worn*. New York: Sports Publishing, 2018.

Romero, Elena. *Free Stylin': How Hip Hop Changed the Fashion Industry*. Santa Barbara, CA: Praeger, 2012.

Shieber, Tom. "Dressed to the Nines: A History of the Baseball Uniform." National Baseball Hall of Fame and Museum, 2003. http://exhibits.baseballhalloffame.org/dressed_to_the_nines/index.htm.

Siegel, Alan. "How Mitchell & Ness Built an Empire and Launched the Golden Age of Sports Nostalgia." *USA Today*, July 15, 2015. https://ftw.usatoday.com/2015/07/throwback-jersey-mitchell-ness-toronto-raptors.

Spalding's Official Base Ball Guide. Saint Louis, MO: Horton, 1882.

Thorn, John. *Treasures of the Baseball Hall of Fame: The Official Companion to the Collection at Cooperstown*. New York: Villard, 1998.

Tynan, Jane, and Lisa Godson, eds. *Uniform: Clothing and Discipline in the Modern World*. New York: Bloomsbury Visual Arts, 2019.

Wolf, Cam. "It's Time to Pull the Baseball Uniform into the 21st Century." *Racked*, April 6, 2017. https://www.racked.com/2017/4/6/15168578/rebuild-baseball-uniform.

Wong, Stephen, and Dave Grob. *Game Worn: Baseball Treasures from the Game's Greatest Heroes and Moment*. Washington, DC: Smithsonian Books, 2016.

PHOTOGRAPHY CREDITS

Rooting for Laundry
Figs. 1–5 Courtesy of Anika Orrock.

Behind the Seams
Fig. 6 Courtesy of Library of Congress, Prints & Photographs Division, LC-DIG-ppmsca-68763. Figs. 7–8 National Baseball Hall of Fame and Museum/Milo Stewart Jr. Fig. 9 Courtesy of the Boston Red Sox. Fig. 10 WENN Rights Ltd/Alamy Stock Photo. Fig. 11 Courtesy of Amy Torbert. Fig. 12 Reproduced from the original held by the Department of Special Collections of the Hesburgh Libraries of Notre Dame. Fig. 13 Shutterstock. Fig. 14 Roshan Spotsville. Fig. 15 © 1989 Universal Photo Credit: David Lee All Rights Reserved File Reference #31623144THA. Fig. 16 Courtesy of Plymouth State University/D&M Collection.

The Modern Jersey
Fig. 18 © 2020 Nike, Inc. All rights reserved. Cat. 1 Courtesy of the American Antiquarian Society. Cat. 2 Reproduced from the original held by the Department of Special Collections of the Hesburgh Libraries of Notre Dame. Cat. 3 Reproduced from the original held by the Department of Special Collections of the Hesburgh Libraries of Notre Dame. Cat. 4 Courtesy of the American Antiquarian Society. Cat. 5. Courtesy of Historic New England. Fig. 19 Harvard University, Harvard University Archives, hua25013c00011. Cats. 6–7 Bennington Museum, Bennington, Vermont. Cat. 15 National Baseball Hall of Fame and Museum/Milo Stewart Jr. Figs. 20–21 Courtesy of the Boston Public Library, Michael T. "Nuf Ced" McGreevy Collection. Cat. 16 Courtesy of Historic New England. Cats. 17–19 Bennington Museum, Bennington, Vermont. Cat. 20 National Baseball Hall of Fame and Museum/Milo Stewart Jr. Fig. 22 SDN-055785, Chicago Sun-Times/Chicago Daily News collection, Chicago History Museum © Sun-Times Media, LLC. All rights reserved. Cat. 22 National Baseball Hall of Fame and Museum/Milo Stewart Jr. Cat. 23 Bennington Museum, Bennington, Vermont. Fig. 23 Courtesy of the Library Congress, Prints &

Photographs Division, LC-B2- 3088-6. Cats. 24–25 Courtesy of the New Hampshire Historical Society. Cat. 26 Courtesy of Historic New England. Cat. 28 Courtesy of the New Hampshire Historical Society. Figs. 24–26 Courtesy of Plymouth State University/D&M Collection. Cat. 29 National Baseball Hall of Fame and Museum/Milo Stewart Jr. Fig. 27 Courtesy of the Boston Public Library, Leslie Jones Collection. Fig. 28 Courtesy of the Boston Red Sox. Cat. 31 National Baseball Hall of Fame and Museum/Milo Stewart Jr. Fig. 29 John W. Mosley Photograph Collection, Charles L. Blockson Afro-American Collection, Temple University Libraries, Philadelphia, Pennsylvania. Cat. 44; Cat. 46 Division of Cultural and Community Life, National Museum of American History, Smithsonian Institution. Cat. 47 National Baseball Hall of Fame and Museum/Milo Stewart Jr. Fig. 30 Courtesy of Saint Vincent College. Cats. 48–50 Courtesy of the artist. Cat. 51 Courtesy of the artist. Cat. 52 Courtesy of the artist and ClampArt, New York City. Cats. 53–60 Courtesy of the artist. Fig. 31 Courtesy of the Boston Red Sox. Fig. 32 Courtesy of the Worcester Red Sox. Cats. 63–64 Courtesy of the artist. Figs. 33–37 Courtesy of the artist.

Experimental Design
Fig. 38 Courtesy of the artist. Cat. 66 National Baseball Hall of Fame and Museum/Milo Stewart Jr. Fig. 41 Courtesy of the Boston Public Library, Leslie Jones Collection. Cat. 67 Courtesy of Historic New England. Fig. 42 Archives & Special Collections Library, Vassar College. Cat. 70 Division of Cultural and Community Life, National Museum of American History, Smithsonian Institution. Fig. 43 Courtesy of Mrs. Janice Lee Stone. Cat. 71 National Baseball Hall of Fame and Museum/Milo Stewart Jr. Cat. 72 © MLB Advanced Media, LP. All rights reserved. Fig. 44 National Baseball Hall of Fame and Museum/Milo Stewart Jr. Cat. 73 Photo by Walter Iooss Jr./Sports Illustrated via Getty Images. Cat. 74 National Baseball Hall of Fame and Museum/Milo Stewart Jr. Cat. 75 © MLB Advanced Media, LP. All rights reserved.

Cat. 76 National Baseball Hall of Fame and Museum/Milo Stewart Jr. Figs. 45–46 Ben VanHouten/Seattle Mariners.

Off the Field
Fig. 47 Kwesi Yanful (@kwesithethird) with Creative Direction by Temi Thomas (@Temithomas_). Fig. 48 Courtesy of the Wentz Family. Cats. 81–82 Courtesy of the artist. Cats. 83–89 © The Topps Company, Inc. All rights reserved. Cats. 90–92 Terry O'Neill/Iconic Images. Cat. 93 Courtesy of FIDM/Fashion Institute of Design & Merchandising. Fig. 49 © Paramount Pictures/Entertainment Pictures. Cats. 94–95 Courtesy of Mitchell & Ness Nostalgia Company. Cats. 96–98 Courtesy of the artist. Cat. 99a–b Courtesy of the artist. Figs. 50–51 Courtesy of the artist. Cat. 100 Courtesy of the artist. Fig. 52 Courtesy of the artist. Cat. 101 Paris, Collection Louis Vuitton. Fig. 53 Photo by Melodie Jeng/Getty Images. Fig. 54 WENN Rights Ltd/Alamy Stock Photo. Cat. 103 Courtesy of Mitchell & Ness Nostalgia Company. Fig. 55 National Baseball Hall of Fame and Museum/Milo Stewart Jr. Cat. 105 Runaway LLC. Fig. 56 Japanese American National Museum (Gift of Mori Shimada, 92.10.2DF). Fig. 57 Jillian Clark. Cats. 106–7; Figs. 58–60 Kwesi Yanful (@kwesithethird) with Creative Direction by Temi Thomas (@ Temithomas_). Fig. 61 Shutterstock. Cats. 109–10 Courtesy of Ashish. Cats. 111–12 Courtesy of the artist.

INDEX

Page numbers in *italics* indicate illustrations and their captions